THE MUSICIAN'S
CAREER GUIDE

THE MUSICIAN'S
CAREER GUIDE

TURNING YOUR TALENT INTO SUSTAINED SUCCESS

ULYSSES OWENS JR.

WITH ARLEN GARGAGLIANO

AFTERWORD BY ALEXANDER SMALLS

ALLWORTH PRESS
NEW YORK

Contents

Letter to the Students

Dear Student,

Congratulations to you! Deciding to take the path of working in the music industry—in any capacity—is a brave and powerful choice, and one that I'm honored to support you in.

To start, I'm going to tell you a bit about myself, and how this book came to be. One of the things I enjoy most about teaching is that I have the opportunity to meet all different people. During my years as an educator at Juilliard, and when I've been out giving talks at schools and conferences, I have had a chance to meet a variety of students who ranged in age, religion, gender, ethnicity, and so on. And I'm happy to say that this learning has been mutual; they've all taught me so much, too. They've brought up a lot of questions and considerations that I had never previously thought of. Here, in *The Musician's Career Guide: Turning Your Talent into Sustained Success,* my goals are to share the questions others have had and to blend those answers with my personal experience, thereby producing what I think is a useful fundamental tool for you as you embark on this very exciting journey into the music industry.

First, I'm going to backtrack a bit and share some of my "lightbulb moments," in the hope that they'll also resonate with you. I remember watching an interview with Quincy Jones where he stated, "We as musicians forget that the music business is a business." He continued to emphasize that being a creative these days is also being a businessperson. All the aspects of a business—scalability, sustainability, growth, vision, and purpose—are necessary to consider when trying to establish oneself as a business entity. I did not always know this, and would like to have recognized it earlier—so I am sharing it with you here.

Second, I'm recounting another eye-opening event: on my first day of ensemble class at the Juilliard School, jazz drum veteran Carl Allen posed this question to our class: "Are you guys interested in making a living or designing a career?"

I immediately raised my hand and asked, "Carl, what's the difference?"

He then said, "Young brother, when you make a living, you are working as a musician and only focusing on what gigs/performances you will take, based solely on the monetary value. However, when you are building a career, you are incredibly strategic about the placement each performance will create for you."

This is also something I didn't realize initially, and will go into more detail about in this book.

These points—and bits of knowledge—are what resonate the most for me even to this day, and something I want to share with you. It's important to have business savvy, and part of that is being strategic. This book will help guide you in both of those areas. Additionally, as a talented, ambitious and creative person, I want you to know these four key points:

- Life is always changing;
- Life is about how you connect with people;
- Life is the sum total of the decisions you make, and what you have the faith and imagination to believe is possible for yourself; and
- You must NEVER QUIT!

I state this, because one of the things that was important about my journey in music is that it started with sheer love: love for the drums, love for playing at church for choirs, and then eventually love for jazz. This love caused me to set goals that made me pursue an education in New York City. However, one of the key things I didn't understand was business. For many years, in traveling and studying,

I have intersected with so many business professionals, and no matter if they are accountants, real estate investors, managers, salespeople, etc., they understand some basic principles of business that many creatives don't either know or focus on. Understanding those principles led me to important questions.

I'm going to address these questions in the book, but to start, I'd like you to take a moment and think about these two different sets of questions:

1. What is my love? What is my talent? What is the current packaging of my love and talent? Am I a brand? Who is consuming it? Is it profitable? Is that profit sustainable and leading to maximum growth?

2. What talent will I choose to hire and create an opportunity for exposure? How much money do I want to invest into this talent? Whom will I choose to manage, endorse, or book? Whom will I sign to a record deal?

What's interesting to me is that these two sets of questions come from different places of power: one is coming from the "talent" and the other is comping from the "decision maker." The talent is often waiting for the decision maker to approve them, while the decision maker has the control and can decide at any moment whom they want to invest in.

Don't worry if this isn't clear yet; I promise you that during the course of this book, it will be. Much of what I will discuss in this book is a changing economic climate that is affecting the shape of the music business for students who are in school right now. This, dear student, is fundamental for your growth and knowledge as an individual who is aspiring to work in this ever-changing, always-inspiring field. It is my hope that you as an artist will dive into this book and find hope and possibility in new career opportunities, and also find agency within yourself and recognize that with hard work, anything is possible.

My goal for this book is to remove the wall between the creative mindset and the business mindset, and to create a dialogue so that musicians can become more business-savvy and aware of realities that will allow for them to be successful. I want this to be a tool for you, no matter what genre or aspect of music you're dedicated to, so that it can help prepare you for this industry, and the entrepreneurial world at large. Additionally, if you're a creative professional already working in this industry, this book can be your resource and help you take your career to the next level.

I remember when I graduated; I walked across the stage at Juilliard, grabbed my degree, went home to my apartment in Harlem, and was suddenly consumed with anxiety. I was scared, confused, and simply didn't know what was the next step to take. This book is the tool I wish I'd had. *The Musician's Career Guide: Turning Your Talent into Sustained Success* gives you concrete assistance in a practical and easy-to-attain manner. This book not only lists steps, but also includes mistakes, challenges, and victories that I have experienced.

Many people in this industry wait until their journey has reached a pinnacle moment to write about it. Unfortunately, many of my predecessors hide the truth behind the mystery of phrases like, "It'll all work out . . ."

In my opinion, that's complete bullshit. We need answers, or at least steps that will lead to answers, to open doors and create possibilities. This book will serve that purpose.

Ready? Let's go!

U

Introduction

When I was a little boy in Jacksonville, in second grade, my teacher asked everyone in my class what they wanted to be when they grew up.

She'd start on one side and go around the room with her question: "Johnnie, what do you want to be?"

"A doctor, Mrs. Cole," Johnnie smiled proudly.

"What about you Nathan?" Mrs. Cole continued.

"A pilot, Mrs. Cole," Nathan declared.

"What about you, Ulysses?" she asked me, though I think even then, she knew what I would say.

"A Drummer, Mrs. Cole," I responded, tapping my desk, as I always did, unconsciously. Even at age seven, I knew that this was my destiny.

I have been playing the drums since I was two years old; I am told I started playing before I could form complete sentences. I hear rhythm in everything: when the windshield wipers are turned on, when raindrops are falling from the sky, when the faucet is dripping, when people are walking, and when the trees sway and the leaves brush together. I define my drumming talent as a gift; though it can be called a skill, it's something that I feel I was born with. Now, when I look back, I can see that there are "extensions" of my gift, though I also call them hobbies or passions: writing, speaking, producing, and more.

As we get started, I want to share a couple of points with you. One is a quote that resonates with me, and the other is a real-life story.

"We delight in the beauty of the butterfly, but rarely admit the changes it has gone through to achieve that beauty."
—Maya Angelou, American Poet, Singer, Memoirist and Civil Rights Activist

What does this quote mean? Basically, it's important for us all to recognize that working towards a significant goal like being a professional in the music industry takes time, energy—and hard work.

Now I'd like to share a story with you: I distinctly knew, even at that moment in time when I was in second grade, that I wanted to be a drummer. More importantly, even though I was child, I understood that my love for music was etched into my identity as well.

How does this translate into your life? Well, stay with me. It's important for all of you reading this book to first be incredibly aware of who you are, not just as a person and what gender and race you identify with, but who are you creatively, because if you cannot decide that, then it's going to be very difficult for you to effectively know whom you will/can collaborate with.

On my Instagram page is a really great interview by the Grammy-winning artist, Robert Glasper. In that interview, he explains a few really powerful points about success and destiny. The first thing he speaks about is that we human beings all have hobbies, and a hobby is simply something that you enjoy. For example, in my case, my hobby is watching documentaries and movies of substance that teach me something, and don't just entertain.

The second thing he spoke about was a passion that we may have. For instance, in my case, I am incredibly passionate about food, and the craftsmanship of food and wine; I'm fascinated by the pairing of the two.

Third, he says that we all have a gift, and the interesting thing about the gift that we all possess is that it's something we don't have to work that hard at because it's simply our gift. As he says, when God has gifted you, very rarely will you have to work to have the gift. The work comes in maintaining the gift, and wanting to expand and grow it.

The last point Robert makes is key: many times, we confuse our passions with our gifts, and we often try to force or draw a level of success to our passion, instead of working in the area of our gift and finding incredible success by utilizing our gifts. He states that we'll find success, or whatever we define as success, much quicker when we spend time working in the area of our divine gifts.

In discovering who you are, I want you to truly understand what your gift is, and separate it from your hobby and even your passion, because when you can work fully in the area of your gift, the ability to thrive and be successful will be present immediately.

Again, I want to share an example with you: writing was something I had been doing since I was a kid; I have always loved writing letters to romantic interests, and also to my friends. I loved writing poetry, and if I cared deeply about someone, I would write a poem for them. Even at the age of seventeen, in my meditation and spiritual practices, which I became very serious about and focused on, I would write prayers and meditative thoughts constantly. Many times, when I was stressed or confused, I would sit down and write about the subject, and find the clarity I sought. This gave me the realization that, in fact, I have the gift of writing. Now, I have to nurture it, and work with amazing writing mentors and coaches to enhance this skill, but I recognize that it's a gift. And furthermore, when I started to consider writing books, it took very little work and convincing to get the right support, because my gift created connections, and doors immediately began opening.

However, this isn't always the case with me. In fact, there are other parts of my career where I have been trying to fit a square peg into a round hole. To this end, I have exhausted myself trying to create success outside "my gift area." This is the case with my role of bandleader—which is one that I'm still evolving in. Though yes, I could always be a leader, being a bandleader didn't happen organically; I was missing a key element that bandleaders need: vision. So, though I was great at building a band, hiring the right members, and performing, I needed to work on the vision aspect and having a sonic identity for my vision—which is something that I'm still developing.

But now I have some questions for your consideration:

- What are your hobbies?
- What is your passion?
- What are your gifts?
- What do you most love?
- What areas or talents come easiest to you?
- How are you currently working in these areas?

These are the questions you need to ask yourself as you embark on this journey.

As I tell my students, success in this industry doesn't come without effort. Yes, it's true: it often seems seamless and simple. But it takes effort, passion, and devotion to make it in any industry—especially in the music industry. Now stay with me here; I want to keep you going— and encourage you, but I am honest, and want to tell you the way it is. Really.

PART 1

YOU ARE A BUSINESS

It's time for you to start to think differently. Yes, this business that you are in—or about to be in—can be daunting, overwhelming, and frustrating. The good news is that you have the resources, and you will soon learn how to channel them. In this section of the book, I encourage you to do some self-reflecting, while offering you tools to maximize your ability to navigate this industry.

CHAPTER 1
Maximize Your Environments

"You arrive at a village, and in this calm environment, one starts to hear echo."—Yannick Noah, French International Tennis Hall of Famer, Singer, Co-founder of Les Enfants de la Terre in 1988 with his mother, and also Fête le Mur, a tennis association for underprivileged children.

The surroundings in which a person operates can have a huge impact on his or her life—positive and negative. As is the case for all of you, throughout the course of my life, I have had various environments that contributed to my current state of being. In my case, I'm lucky to have always had a community of supporters around me who encouraged me through the joys and challenges of my environment: the various institutions, bands, and training grounds. As an aspiring musician, or someone just diving into the music industry, it's crucial that you recognize your environment. I'm going to start by telling you about the four environments that have shaped me as a professional drummer, as well as lessons I'd like to share with you. Before I start, I want to tell you something: it's important to make the best of whatever environment you are in, and if you so choose to create your own environment, make sure you remain connected to the larger world—the one beyond your world.

MY FIRST ENVIRONMENT: CHURCH

For most musicians, particularly in the African-American diaspora, church is their first introduction to a music school, and in many ways, it is a conservatory. I grew up being introduced to music at the Steele and Blue Church of God, in Jacksonville, Florida, where I was initially exposed to the sound of gospel music. Thanks to my mother, who served as choir director, I was placed near the drum set as a young child so that she could watch me and make sure I wasn't getting into trouble. One time, when the drummer had left the drum set for a break, I climbed up and stood—because I was just two and couldn't reach the stool—then picked up his sticks and began to keep time. At that time, before I could even put together a complete sentence, my family took note of my skills. They continued to encourage me to keep playing, and despite my very young age, gave me the opportunity to play music any time it was available. This was incredibly cool because it allowed me to fall in love with music in the most natural way: with no rules attached.

When I was about eight years old, the church drummer left. At that moment, the church had a decision to make: either search for a new drummer, or give this kid a chance to play. Well, they opted for the latter. At age eight, I suddenly had the chance—the privilege—to play for three choirs, and attend several rehearsals weekly. This coupled with my mom's constant reminders about this opportunity being a privilege, and that God could have chosen anyone to give this gift to, but that I was the lucky recipient, and that I should respectfully honor this with my faithfulness and humility. This lesson, learned within this environment, has continued to last a lifetime for me—even beyond church. My message to you? Always be humbled and grateful for being chosen for an opportunity. The lesson of faithfulness even within an environment where there was no great monetary value was really special for me, because it taught me to learn how to be committed solely for the sake of commitment, not based on an immediate monetary reward.

MY SECOND ENVIRONMENT: MIDDLE SCHOOL

The second environment that was pivotal to my development was my middle school, James Weldon Johnson College Preparatory Middle, also in Jacksonville. It was there that I first worked with Mrs. Gail Henley, a wonderful band director. She was the first person to tell me that I needed to focus and take my drumming gift seriously. When I met her at the James Weldon Johnson summer band camp, I showed up with an alto saxophone, because I had grown tired of playing the drums. She heard me play the sax, and kindly asked if I played another instrument. When I told her I played the drums, she asked me to go to the drum set and play. I played some grooves for her. When I stopped, she requested I come back to the front of the room, and speak with her.

"Ulysses," Mrs. Henley began, "Please take that saxophone home, and never return with it." I looked at her, politely, but very surprised by her request.

She continued, "You are going to be my drummer. I'll also teach you classical percussion as well as marching band percussion. Your percussion talent is what is needed in my band."

THE LESSON FOR YOU?

Despite the fact that we can have an idea of what our talent could be, we need to focus on areas where we can surely thrive. I'm thankful always to Mrs. Henley for guiding and teaching me that lesson. Otherwise, I would be too caught up in my own head, where I think my greatest value lies. So, it's great to trust others, and if a job or opportunity needs what is in you, then follow in that direction.

MY THIRD ENVIRONMENT: HIGH SCHOOL

At my parents' insistence, and despite my initial reaction, I attended Douglas Anderson School of the Arts for high school. This, as I later realized that my parents had recognized, was the best thing in the world for me, because it introduced and exposed me to the world that

I would spend the rest of my life in. I was initially reluctant, because I was a bit afraid to really be around the tribe that I was called to, which was the artists. I was not really taking myself seriously, because though I knew I was talented, I didn't know if I was really ready to fully commit to that journey and be part of the artistic community. Thank God for smart parents, because the minute I stepped foot on campus, I truly felt peace. I was surrounded by like-minded individuals.

There were many lessons I learned in school, and many of them are woven into this book. My high school academic environment taught me one lesson in particular that I want to share with you here:

When I was a freshman, I started to let my grades slide. I was coming, after all, from a situation in which I even if my grades slipped, they would always let me perform. Well, DASotA, I soon learned, was a different story. I started failing in algebra. I subsequently suffered two big blows: I was placed on academic probation and wasn't allowed to perform for the longest nine-week period ever. When I whined about it, the jazz band director told me that my lack of academic excellence failed the band, and that I should realize how much my absence would affect the band.

After that, I never failed a subject.

This lesson for you? Well, actually there are two: One, it's important to keep up with all aspects of your education. Two, you are part of a team when you're in a band, and your performance affects everyone.

MY FOURTH ENVIRONMENT: COLLEGE

First, I will tell you a little bit about how I even discovered what Juilliard was.

I was hanging out in the guidance counselor's office at Douglas Anderson School of the Arts, and I saw this really colorful and thick book with the bold title, *Juilliard*, written across it. I asked someone what it was, and they said that it was one of the best schools in the world for talented artists. I subsequently learned that Juilliard had a donor that created a program called The Juilliard Experience, which was basically an opportunity geared towards boosting minority enrollment, particularly amongst African-American and Latinx students. I applied, and got accepted during my eleventh and twelfth grade years of high school. This experience gave me the chance to visit Juilliard for three days and shadow a current student.

This opportunity changed my life. I realized that I loved that environment; I felt "at home" with students who were completely submerged in their experience—and, for the first time, I no longer felt like the weird guy that obsesses over his love for music. After those visits, plus many hours of practice and preparation, I was accepted into the Inaugural Jazz Studies Program at Juilliard and awarded a full scholarship with a stipend and a chance to make history as the first African-American jazz drummer to ever enter the school in its over 100 years of existence.

Being at Juilliard was also unique because I was surrounded by some of the most talented students in the world, and I also felt like the worst student there in terms of talent. All of my colleagues were jazz babies, and had been exposed to records and live concerts of jazz masters for many years. On the other hand, I had only seen a few live jazz concerts with legends. I also felt that I had such a small album collection in comparison to the other students. It was so funny because this era was pre-MP3s, so all of the musicians in the Juilliard Jazz program would have listening sessions and we would judge ourselves based on our CD collection, and how many CD binders we had, which was representative of how much music we were listening to, which ultimately determined how great of a musician we were.

The level of intensity of the musicianship, and artistry of all students in all departments, was amazing and always pushed me to be better. I am always thankful when I show up and I am the worst person in the room, because it means that I have a long way to go and a lot to learn.

Lastly, all the Juilliard faculty members are world-class artists, so it's incredibly easy to just be connected to who is relevant on the music scene; I was constantly inspired during my life as a student there.

This lesson? Well, actually, there are two lessons here, too: One, it's important to keep your eyes open, because you never know what opportunities can present themselves to you, and two, go to college!

This last lesson leads me into the next section, which is all about college. This is an environment that you may not be in yet, but one you should most certainly get into.

PURSUE YOUR COLLEGE DEGREE

Whether or not you've finished high school, I know that if even if you've had some success as a creative, you might start to doubt the value of college. Well, let me tell you that college is a hugely important and crucial step in your training. If you want to pursue mastery, or if you just want to become great on a certain level, then continue the route that you are pursuing. Even those that have become celebrities always speak about taking the time to develop their skill-set at a higher level.

In my case, Juilliard was the environment that honed my training; it allowed me to know what it is to be surrounded by the best. For those reading this who want to be the best, place yourself in an environment where *that* is the status quo. I did not learn how to be jazz drummer at Juilliard, because I walked into the school with that talent and understanding. What I did learn at Juilliard was how to be a professional musician and a thinking artist. Additionally, within that environment, they allowed me to build a huge artistic network that spans the globe. Lastly, Juilliard opened up my imagination, and I no longer see the world artistically as a place with limits; I have a fully limitless imagination. Now the goal has become finding the resources to create what I envision. Lucky for you, there are many places and colleges where this energy can be found and can inspire you as well.

Because there are so many options when it comes to college, choosing can be challenging. Consider what colleges fit your level of talent; potential growth is an element not to be taken lightly. Again, I share my experience: I had a few goals before college, and one goal was to move to New York City, because I felt that if I could move to NYC, I would be surrounded by the best, and by default, my skill set would have to rise to meet the occasion of those around me. Sink or swim is constantly the way that I test myself and force growth. Pursuing Juilliard was definitely a goal that forced me to see what and how I needed to adjust to get ready—and I will address that in a moment. But first, another suggestion for you: if you're not sure where to attend college, do consult your guidance counselor and/or mentors in your life. Even if you think you have an idea, their suggestions can only complement your investigations.

PAY ATTENTION TO YOUR COLLEGE APPLICATION

Given the various educational positions that I have been fortunate to hold, and my own experience as a student, I have witnessed so many mistakes that applicants make during this process. Here is some relevant advice for you. Currently, because of the confidentiality of my job, I can only speak about this to a certain point, but I can share some key advice based upon what I have seen:

Take the process seriously

Pre-screening for an audition is the opportunity for the faculty to determine if you qualify for a live audition, something you should obviously want. For highly competitive schools, this is a "weeding out" process to make sure the pool of applicants is qualified enough for potential acceptance. Therefore, you must be prepared.

Pay attention to details

It's important to make sure that you pay attention to every aspect of the college application. Take the time to fill out the application correctly. Follow the instructions. Often students are asked to write personal statements. Get someone who is skilled in writing to help you craft these personal statements so you can effectively articulate your goals. There is nothing more powerful than a faculty member hearing from a student about why he or she is striving to attend their school's program. Make sure yours accurately reflects you. After all, this is part of your first impression and potential entrée into the school. Look at everything carefully.

Take the time to read through—and read through again. These instructions also pertain to repertoire: for those that are recording with rhythm sections, and other musicians, make sure that they are prepared and take this as seriously as you do.

Have a reputable teacher

Make sure you choose a teacher that has either taken the path you are trying to follow, or is in some way connected to the school you wish to attend. There is a standard of excellence and talent that every school will accept; your teacher must be the one to successfully guide you prior to the audition, with tips to carry you through the experience. I have often seen pre-screen audition candidates where a student has no musical clue on how to approach the audition. A good teacher will make sure you a have the ability and skills to perform your piece(s). Do your homework: research your teacher's qualifications and track record. If your teacher can't take you there, get a new teacher.

Use proper equipment to record yourself and practice, practice, practice

Some colleges may require a personal interview. Take the time and use the right kind of camera to film yourself in order to practice. Additionally, make sample recordings so that you can see how you're coming across, and make changes accordingly. I can't emphasize enough the importance of preparation in this aspect. As you may or may not realize, faculty can easily tell when an applicant is not ready to perform pieces, and can barely make it through their audition process. Obviously, you don't want this to happen to you.

Understand the live audition

As a musician, one of the things you'll have to prepare for is the live audition—both in college and beyond—but let's start with college.

In my case, this was a new area for me, and I knew I needed some help in order to get ready. After all, I had made up my mind: I was going to go to Juilliard. But now I had to successfully pass my live audition so that I could be accepted. The first thing I wanted to do was to get professional advice. I pursued several musicians who were not only stellar musicians, but also excellent educators. I went to each of them, and asked their opinions about what I needed to work on musically. I put myself into a six-month system of training to sharpen my musical breadth along with my career preparation. I wanted to make sure that I would be familiar with all of the requirements that they would ask of me; I didn't want any of them to be foreign to me. That was just the musical side. Then I met with several people to assist in me with updating my résumé and my bio. The first part of the audition was based on the pre-screened tape, which I spoke about earlier. Once I heard back from them that my pre-screened audition was accepted, and I was invited to a live audition, I had to take it to the next level.

There's no spoiler alert here; you all know that I passed! But what I do want to share this advice so that you can pass.

These four steps, in addition to what was listed for the pre-screening process, will guide you in the preparation for YOUR college audition(s)—and auditions beyond, as well:

1) Dress appropriately.

People still judge a book by its cover. I remember at my college audition, I showed up in a sports jacket, tie, and freshly shined shoes. I remember being in the hallways, and many of the applicants were laughing at me. Many of them were older, because it was the first year of the Juilliard Jazz auditions and the program had not been fully accredited yet, so I was in the pool of auditions with applicants almost twice my age and experience. That said, once I was accepted one of the administrators told my mother and I how much it meant to the panel that I took the time to dress up and be presentable during my interview and audition. Dressing up appropriately—along with preparation—shows that this opportunity matters to you.

2) Do your research.

Speak to an alumnus or current student. As always, it's key to consult others who have the knowledge; this case is no different. It's incredibly important to speak with people who have come before you in the program, and seek their advice regarding the audition process. In my case, though no one had come before me in this particular audition process, I was still able to get some help: several of the faculty members who were conducting the auditions had been faculty at other institutions. I made sure to speak to people who knew of them and asked them to tell me something about their personality or what to expect from them in that scenario; this was a huge help as far as my preparation. Now I serve as faculty at a few different schools and my bosses constantly advise the faculty members to engage with potential students to guide them during this process. After all, it makes our job—as the audition panel—easier if we encounter students who are prepared and who understand that culture of the institution.

3) Be ready.

This point probably seems redundant, but you'd be surprised at how many applicants have not done adequate preparation for their live audition. Remember, simply being talented does not qualify you for an opportunity; you need to be ready as far as knowledge and practice. I mentioned the term culture as it applies to the institution, and want to explain that more. Every university, conservatory and college, for better or worse, has a culture: a way that the administration, faculty, and students are encouraged to behave and learn in that environment. This culture ultimately impacts your education and the results you receive from your education. Therefore, it's imperative, prior to your audition, to make sure that you are aware of the culture of the school so that you can try to mirror some of that in your choices and preparation.

And finally:

4) Have multiple choices.

I know I said that I had my heart set on Juilliard, but I did have a Plan B—and I recommend you do the same. When you're looking into schools, take into consideration the geographic location, the student body, and the alumni success rate. Also examine potential scholarship opportunities; these may or may not be tied into the school, and require some well-worth-it investigation on your part. One of the big non-negotiable factors for me was the faculty, and I urge you to look into this as well. If you have a faculty that has a career profile that is representative of what you want, then pursue that. However, if your goal is to be a performing artist and most of the faculty are solely academics, then you may want to re-think your choice. The best fit for you—the place where you can grow to be your best self, both musically and beyond—is not the best fit for everyone. This being said, there is always more than one place where you can thrive.

Now, I was pretty bold and I technically only applied to three schools. If I had it my way, I would have only applied to Juilliard, but at the urging of my family, I applied to two other schools. Being purposeful and intentional is a good thing; this, after all, is a huge part of my own psychological and spiritual identity. However, there are multiple roads that can lead to your future successes and endeavors, so, as my grandma used to say, don't put all your eggs in one basket.

5) Be excellent.

Once you've made your choice and been accepted, it's time to address your focus. When speaking to a colleague of mine, and discussing advice for students, the first thing we said was, "Students need to be excellent students." Excellence is a must. When you operate with excellent behavior, people take notice. Take the time to consider this goal in every aspect of your education. As a former student and current faculty member, I'd like to define what this means:

- Show up on time to class.
- Turn your homework in on time, or early if you can.
- Communicate effectively with your teachers.
- Honor your word.
- Be honest.

Nothing replaces excellence, and you will forever be remembered for your effort as a student, because it costs nothing to be consistent, but you'll gain everything from it.

FINISH YOUR COLLEGE DEGREE

"Be exceptionally educated."—Wynton Marsalis, Virtuoso Trumpeter, Composer, Teacher, Artistic Director of Jazz at Lincoln Center and Director of Juilliard Jazz

This quote from Wynton Marsalis says a lot. You may have heard it before, but I'm saying it again: stay in school. Get your degree!

Mastery, a skill you will begin the process of gaining in college, is also a huge component in success. Mastery also truly separates you from others. So much of what is promoted today is a lack of depth in this skill, and more of instantaneous success. However, those who maintain success, and have sustainability and longevity, have been on a path of mastery. Mastery allows your talent to constantly be evolving over time and not just built to capitalize on one moment in time. Mastery will sustain you over multiple decades, and through changes in music. I will talk about this more in Chapter 18, but, dear students, always keep mastery in mind.

Finishing your college degree as a performer, especially someone that needs money and needs to figure out how to make a living, can be quite difficult, and I had a strong temptation to drop out of school. At one point, I actually proceeded with dropping out.

I was in my third year of college, my career had started to take off, and I was being hired consistently by several influential jazz musicians and started touring regularly. I thought to myself, "Most great jazz musicians that I admired never went to college, or definitely didn't finish college, so why am I stressing about it?" So I told my family that I was going to drop out and just settle on getting an artist's diploma, and that would be all that I needed.

I went to the registrar's office, submitted the paperwork, and was planning to finish the second semester and begin my journey as freelance jazz musician. As one of the four high school students that they had let in at Juilliard as part of the inaugural jazz program, I felt comfortable with this choice, because one of my other colleagues had made the same decision.

Then, I changed my mind. Marcus Baylor, dear friend and accomplished drummer, had some inspirational words for me. In fact, his words are why I chose to go back and finish my degree. He said, "Ulysses, the road will always be there, trust me, it ain't going nowhere. However, the opportunity to finish your degree won't always be there, because there will be specific moments in your life where you simply won't have the time nor energy that you have now to commit to this. Lastly, you don't know where your career will lead you; the opportunities to do other things beyond playing may present themselves to you."

These words—golden and monumental advice—are what I want to pass on to you. This was truly invaluable guidance, and every time I see Marcus, and his lovely wife, Jean, I give them big hugs thanks to their tremendous advice. As a result of the push they gave me, my career has definitely involved more than just playing. As they predicted, my college degree has aided me in so many valuable ways. Yes, be aware that though a college education may not be as important for your playing, it may be crucial for other things that are unknown in your future. I had no idea when I graduated college that I would end up starting an organization for inner-city kids where I would have to utilize my college degree daily. The fact that I completed my degree appeals to future donors, supporters, and grantees.

In conclusion, maximizing your college environment plays a huge role in your life as a musician, and what you do within that environment is just as important, if not more. Be mindful of that, and craft your environment as needed. For some, it will not be within a college that they pursue mastery; it may be in the "school of hard knocks," and being educated solely by experience, which is great as well. This is the old-school way, and particularly as a jazz musician, so much of our music and mastery in jazz is accomplished outside of the classroom, because it wasn't born in school, it was born in the street. Really learning how to connect to an audience and make your music matter in the world, while discovering your own unique voice, will not occur in a collegiate environment.

In conclusion, environment plays a huge role in your life as a musician. Be mindful of that, and craft your environment as needed. This will help you define and ultimately succeed at attaining your goals.

Reflections for thought and discussion:

1. What are the available resources in your current environment?
2. How are you being challenged?
3. Are you focusing on an area in which you can thrive?
4. Are you on a path of mastery?
5. Do you have a teacher that can help you grow and support your goals?
6. Do you have any auditions coming up? If so, are you fully prepared?

Reflections for writing:

1. List three advantages of your current environment.
2. List three challenges of your current environment.
3. List resources that will allow you to work through the challenges you've listed, and subsequently experience more advantages within this environment. Write concrete steps you can take to make this happen.

CHAPTER 2
Career Profile

"Do you want to make a living or design a career?"—Carl
Allen, Jazz Drummer, Educator, Clinician, Bandleader

In the last chapter, I addressed the importance that college plays in your professional career. As Carl's quote illustrates, there is much more. Here and now, we need to move on to another element for your consideration: your career profile. This is different for everyone, especially within jazz, where you have educators, producers, sidemen, and leaders, and so many other types of careers that are yet to be discovered. In this chapter, I define what I call some basic career profile types, and also give you more food for thought as far as the timing commitment you want to make, partnered with your mindset about this industry and your potential role in it.

When I was in college, my main goal was to be a sideman drummer. To prepare myself, I went to all of the gigs that featured my teachers: Carl Allen, Lewis Nash, Billy Drummond, and Herlin Riley. This helped me to deepen my understanding about how their careers worked. For example, it allowed me to examine what they were looking for in musicians that played with them, and what was necessary for me to achieve so that I could at least try to work towards all they had accomplished. This observing my role models also helped me to consider and define what I wanted out of my own career.

Now it's time for *you* to think about what you might want.

What I have listed here below are some basic career profile types that I've worked within. My goal is to increase your awareness and, ideally, spark your interest. These roles, by the way, are neither complete nor mutually exclusive: you certainly may have a career profile outside this listing or, as I've done, have more than one career profile. In any case—here are a few, with some relevant information:

Bandleader

This is essentially the role that most musicians desire to fulfill, because it places them not only at the front of the stage, but also fully in charge and accountable for everything that moves the vision of their band forward.

I remember being in college with this really talented musician. When he was seventeen years old, he was a freshman at Juilliard. He started out, and from the first day I met him, with a vision for himself as a musician and, in particular, as a bandleader. Almost immediately, he began to assemble a band to move forward the agenda that he had. It was fascinating to witness his effect on people even back then! Well, this young talented musician worked through college, and continued to establish his brand, and focus his vision. That musician's name is Jon Batiste, and he's currently the bandleader for Stephen Colbert's *Late Show*, where he consistently demonstrates to an audience of hundreds of thousands his range, influences—and great skill.

The interesting thing about being a bandleader is that some people are just born with that ability, while some of us (me included) have to work hard to focus our sound and musical aesthetic to establish what our musical identity is as a bandleader. For me, being a bandleader has been a journey. I have spent many years as a sideman supporting many musicians; taking charge is a welcome—but new and often-challenging—role.

Composer

A composer is primarily a person who composes music. The great Vincent Herring stated that being a composer is something that every musician should cultivate not just because it gives one great pleasure, but also because of publishing and ownership. Additionally, being a composer, especially if your music gets licensed by a major show or network, can be a major revenue stream.

Though composing not been my strongest suit, it is something that I hope to venture deeper into later in life, when I am on the road less, and have the time to dedicate myself to the study and focus needed in order to successfully translate my musical ideas into compositions.

Educator

Since very early in my career, I have simultaneously been a professional musician and an educator. As my skill and knowledge for my craft increased, so did the number of students who wanted to learn from me. This helped me hone my own teaching approach and the accompanying philosophy.

One of the key things I want to advise all musicians is that they should make sure that they work on their ability to articulate their pedagogy and technical proficiency. As you probably recognize, just because you can do something doesn't mean you can teach it. This is true also in the realm of music; many musicians can play, but not many can teach what and how they play.

Personally, education has become a passion; it's opened up a way for me to not only deal with personal challenges, but also the possibility of broadening my borders and opportunities as a musician. As a result of teaching, I have enjoyed unique opportunities around the world. I've had the privilege of taking my knowledge about jazz and sharing it with others in Asia, the Middle East, Africa, Europe, and beyond. This kind of teaching, as I've mentioned before, benefits both the learner and the teacher; it's a mutually beneficial—and enjoyable—venture.

Philanthropist

My passion for philanthropy was something that I quite honestly had not counted on. Though I was raised with an ideology that giving to others was important, I never thought I would someday incorporate that into my professional life. Today, along with my family, we have one philanthropic organization that devotes time and capital to the education of children in the realm of the arts. Because of the meaningful nature of this crucial work, I am especially and eternally thankful for it. Furthermore, it's educational for me, too; my kids and staff constantly teach me so much.

Producer

In the music industry, a producer is also a project manager; you have to be organized and know how to move forward with a cohesive plan and in a timely manner. Great producers know how to tap into the musical desire and vision of the artist, and help them to formulate, articulate, and focus on their vision. Secondly, they know whom to call—whom to bring into the room in order to bring the musical vision to life. And finally, they know how to, via their musical knowledge paired with business acumen, make a musical product that will stand the test of time and bring it to completion. Most producers, in my opinion, are glorified project managers, and if they don't have the ability to create timelines along with the creative side, it's going to be difficult to manifest a product.

My steps in this direction had a couple of catalysts. Greg Knowles, my mentor, told me years ago, "Kid, you got some big ears musically, and I think you could be a great producer if you invested your time and energy into the craft." Then, when fellow Juilliard alum and jazz bassist Matthew Rybicki asked me about recording his first album, I mentioned that I wanted to get into producing, and offered to produce it at no cost; I realized that this way I could learn, and he could reach his goal without losing money!

The result was a great one: not only did he love my work, but others did as well. We got great reviews from major jazz publications. This set me out on my next producing path. I started to research great producers, and even seek out producing mentors. Now, over nine years later, my company, U.O.J. Productions, has produced over forty records globally for major record labels.

At this point, I've learned a tremendous amount about being a music producer, and have developed my own rules for being a great one. Here are my top three:

1. Music producers must be musicians. I don't think you can be a "beat maker" or simply great at navigating computer software and call yourself a music producer. You have to know something about music. By having this knowledge, you not only become more effective in achieving your goal, you also eliminate your clients' limitations and expectations.

2. Music producers must be good with people. Because you are constantly the front guy/gal, and dealing with so many different people, you need to be able to get along well with others.

3. Music producers must be great at simultaneously navigating the intricacies of many relationships. Beyond just getting along, you must be able to manage many. For example, on any given album, I manage between twenty-five and thirty relationships between the band, engineers, studios, arrangers, and more. Conversely, if the producer can't be trusted with managing these relationships successfully, they will be a hindrance to the artist and the project.

Sideman (Sideperson)

When I first entered this business at sixteen years old, I was functioning in the capacity of a jazz side musician, which essentially is a person who shows up and gets hired to make the bandleader's musical dreams come true. It's a sideman's job to learn the music, be prepared, and also constantly say yes to the needs of the bandleader. In fact, when you choose this position, you do it because you are in the mindset of serving the bandleader; he or she deserves to have your full dedication and commitment.

There are, additionally, rules for being a successful and respected sideman/side-person. In fact, if, as a jazz sideman/side-person, you don't follow these rules—including making sure you know the tune (if you don't know it, read it!) and being prepared—and more, you will not be invited back to perform.

I speak from experience: there was an artist I worked for, and, at the time, I was managing a few different relationships as a sideman in various bands. I didn't have the time to really learn the bandleader's music to the best of my ability, and I assumed that in rehearsal, I would have time to put the music together. But I didn't. I was fired. Almost immediately, someone who was a better musical fit—and who was willing to put in the time to learn that artist's music—was hired.

As I mentioned previously, commitment is key. And along that vein, and that of career profiles, I want to talk about the exciting aspect of this commitment: you get to work hard and constantly look for new ways to re-invent and ultimately sustain yourself. Yes, this can be incredibly exhausting. After all, to be in this business, you definitely need to be a risk-taker, and willing to gamble and bet on yourself. Having faith, and the ability and courage never to quit, is what will lead to the many dimensions of success that you will have. You will experience extreme highs, and challenging lows. BUT, if you are so inclined, I encourage you to go for it; you will find ultimate satisfaction and joy in so many aspects of this profession!

Make sure that, as a side-person, you always stay in touch with your own personal artistic and career goals, dreams, and ambitions, and don't bury them inside of someone else's gig. Have courage and be committed to them, but also be committed to yourself. The goal for each of you is to decide what you desire for yourself, and not feel as though your life is the sum total of what others decide for you.

In conclusion, I can't help but think of one of my role models, the legendary bassist Ron Carter. His career profile began by being a sideman, composer, then an educator, and for the last few decades, he has been a bandleader and has toured the world with his various groups.

He's carved out his own balanced and fruitful life. He generously shares his advice with other musicians about investments and other business-relevant points.

Now it's your turn to consider what level of value you would like to place around your gift. Of course, this can change as you grow, but it's a great place to start.

Reflections for thought and discussion:

1. Which career profile/profiles can you see yourself in?
2. Are there any that you would like to do immediately—and others you'd like to do later? Which ones? Explain.
3. For each one, write what it is about that profile that attracts you.
4. What do you perceive are your strong points to handle these profiles?
5. Do you desire ownership or security?

Reflections for writing:

1. What will be the most challenging aspects of the profiles you're interested in? Write them down.
2. For each challenge, write at least one resolution.
3. What resources do you have readily available to support you? Write down three.
4. If you don't have resources readily available, how will you find them?
5. Who are musicians whose career profiles you identify with? Write down at least three.

CHAPTER 3

What Musicians Need to Know about Business

"This is the Music BUSINESS, so it's important to learn how to effectively do business."—Quincy Jones (Quincy Delight Jones Jr.), Record Producer, Songwriter, Composer, Arranger, Multi-instrumentalist, Film and Television Producer

As a musician, there's often an imbalance between your ability to practice your craft and your knowledge of the music business. Many people automatically assume that choosing to be a musician immediately means giving up or avoiding business altogether, or accepting that the business element of your career is doomed for failure. This doesn't have to be—and shouldn't be—the case. In fact, I'd say it's the opposite: you must not give up nor avoid business; again, I suggest that you *do* need to become business-savvy. Now, I will be touching on this point a lot during this book, but here are my first sets of tips.

It's necessary to understand the fundamentals of business, and to learn how to apply that to your art. Let's start with you.

THREE BASIC BUSINESS FUNDAMENTALS—FOR YOU AS AN INDIVIDUAL

Here are some tips I want to share as it relates to your individual navigation of the music business.

Commit to your word

An agreement for work is firm and shouldn't be changed. When someone hires you for a job, you should do it—and do it well. No exceptions. If
you can't do it, don't accept the job. However, of course life happens, and
there can be emergency situations that might prevent you from keeping
your commitment; this still means you need to honor your word. How
do you do this? Well, if your commitment hast to be changed, there
must be a conversation between the owner, or whomever is in charge on
how to rectify this change. Honesty is always the best policy, and will
allow you to maintain the business relationship. No matter how bad the
issue seems, be honest and it will allow you to maintain your integrity.

Document your discussions and agreements

My mentor, Randy Hall, would often say, "In God We Trust; everyone
else should bring data." It's important to document everything, and
keep a paper trail for all transactions. This is to protect yourself; it's
easy for people to change their story or commitment. Immediately
following a meeting or discussion about work, put your understanding into writing, and send it to the party with whom you've had the
meeting. We will discuss emails, as well as legalities, later in this book,
but in the meantime, I can't stress how crucial documentation is.

Handle yourself in a professional manner

Within business situations, even if it involves family and friends, it's
important to always be professional and behave in a way that puts
your emotions aside. *Being professional* encompasses the use and balance of honesty, restraint, and good character, and we'll go deeper
into that shortly, but right now, I want to share an anecdote with you.

I remember being in the midst of negotiating a deal, and the person who was assigned to work with me, someone I consider a really
great friend, quoted a fee that I simply could not afford. I became
emotional: I was offended because despite the fact that the person
knew about my financial situation, they were still asking for a sum
beyond my means. I spoke to another friend, who said, "You shouldn't
be upset; business is business." That friend advised me to be honest

about what I could afford, and I was. The friendship has grown stronger because I chose not to take things personally. Again, I urge you to repeat this mantra after me: business is business.

BASIC BUSINESS FUNDAMENTALS— FOR YOU AS YOUR OWN BUSINESS MANAGER

You don't need an MBA to function in this industry, but you do need to grasp the basic elements of management. When David S. Hargrett, the founder and principal of Affective Music, a cutting-edge artist management company, was asked about success for people in the music industry, he shared this advice: As someone who routinely books and hires talent, at the forefront of consideration is their reputation: Are they easy to work with? Will they be on time? Will they come prepared? And are they down for the cause? Meaning, how much will they connect to the overall goal? His message for students: talent will get you the chair, your character will keep you there. His good friend and business coach shared a framework with him that I'm sharing here. The way to build and maintain character is by maintaining these key traits: honesty, integrity, and punctuality.

Below are some key areas that you need to develop an understanding of in order to succeed.

People

Navigating people, and understanding them, is key. Learning how to relate to others and build relationships is a basic element for your success. As you probably already know, there will always be certain challenges in dealing with people. After all, we are all human! However, you, as a professional musician and manager, will need to be able to listen, communicate, and, at times, mediate. Having the ability to master these three skills will help you work with people, and ultimately soar in your career.

Operations

In addition to navigating people, you need to navigate the operations aspect of your business. First and foremost, recognize that you are an entity as soon as you start to be a business. Therefore, you need to learn and understand the inner workings of a company or project. The comprehension of operations can only be reached by focusing; you must be constantly engaged in the business, and recognize this—your business— as a priority. Focus will lead you to grasping the many elements in operations. This understanding will prove extremely valuable in your success.

Accounting

Money in and money out is how businesses succeed, survive, or tank. Finance—the continual operation/analysis of how the business will stand on its own—is also fundamentally crucial.

Part of understanding operations is getting the financial end of it, too. You need to comprehend some aspects of accounting and keep track of your own resources and spending. There are a lot of relevant details (like taxes and the IRS) and relevant responsibilities that you need to have reflected in your "books." Having an accountant—a person or department that manages the accounting for your business— is key to not only the survival of the business, but also in defining its financial planning.

Strategy

Speaking of planning, we need to address strategy. As musicians, we go through a few stages of survival with our craft. One of the places we get stuck is when we are working steadily and comfortably on a job; that is when we often cease to think ahead. Developing a next-step strategy, or figuring out what's next, will help you stay ahead of the curve. Actually, my fellow musicians, this is an exciting part our lives, because it's here when we can channel our creativity and pair it with our goals—or what we would like our lives to be. We have options! Think smart within a business context; think of ideas that would work for you as a business, and examine them. Developing strategy will help you plan ahead and, again, be successful. A quick note: everything you do won't work out perfectly, but it's important— as you know—to get out there and keep trying. You will get many things right if you focus and consider carefully.

Marketing

Strategy also transfers into the area of marketing. Previous genera-tions were loyal to businesses for a myriad of reasons. However today, thanks to social media and online businesses, marketing is even more crucial. We'll talk more about social media in a bit, but in the mean-time, let's think about how you choose to advertise and promote your business. Let's face it: there's a lot of talent out there, and you want YOUR idea and business to succeed. Therefore, you need to under-stand that how you choose to advertise and promote your business is key, and a huge component of how your business will grow. In my case, though I've always had some ideas, I've also—as in other areas that I'm not an expert in—involved various team members in the topic of marketing for my business.

Just as a reminder, I want to emphasize: you don't need to be an expert in all of these areas, but you do need to know when and from whom to get expertise.

BASIC FUNDAMENTALS OF BUSINESS ETIQUETTE

Just as important as getting a footing in the more technical aspects of business is understanding the relevant elements of proper etiquette. Just as previously explained, there needs to be science as to how, why, when, and what you choose to do in business. This extends into the realm of etiquette. Here, dear students, I'm including some tips for you to keep in mind.

COMMUNICATE EFFECTIVELY— AND IN A TIMELY MANNER!

One of the keys to success is communication—and I add prompt communication.

I have major issues when people are conducting business with me and they take a long time to respond. Now if people truly want to do business with me, they'll respond promptly. If not, well, I'll pay some-one else who will respond in a timely fashion.

To this end, I'd like to share a quote and an example:

"Many are called, but few pick up the phone."—Donald Lawrence, Gospel Music Songwriter and Record Producer

Dear students, you need to pick up the phone!

Now the example: one of my colleagues, who runs a major program, asked me for a recommendation for someone to hire. I suggested someone who I thought was tailor-made for the opportunity. My colleague subsequently reached out to this person via Facebook, and then called him three times, but the call was never returned.

Later, this same colleague asked for a recommendation, and I suggested this person again; I was unaware that my colleague had tried to reach out but was left without a response.

When I spoke to my colleague, he told me what had happened as far as the lack of response. He said, "Ulysses, I can't beg a person to call me back so I can hire them."

That's when I realized two key points: one, I can want something for someone, but if they don't desire it themselves, then it really doesn't matter; two, and this is the key point here, seize the opportunity when someone calls or contacts you, and respond soon. It can make the difference in getting—or not getting—a great gig.

BE ON TIME!

Speaking of timely responses, I have to mention punctuality. My professor Victor Goines always said to me, "Ulysses, being early is being on time." This is something that is very important to me—and something I want to pass along to you. The way people manage time reflects how they respect other people's time. When someone is constantly late to business meetings, it makes me realize that this person might not be on time for any of our interactions.

I once heard a story about a really famous music director who hired a famous jazz band to participate in an event. The music director, who prided himself on his punctuality, had announced that the downbeat was at 1:00 p.m. However, when the famous jazz band *started* strolling onto the stage at one, he told them, "I know all of you are wonderful, however, I will fire and replace each one of you if you are not ready to play on time," and walked off the stage.

That said, he never had the problem again.

Of course, there will be times when people show up late due to unforeseen circumstances. However, it's my belief that even when those situations arise, if you have been—as I'm suggesting—on time, you will have built up such a reputation that people will give you a level of grace when that happens.

BE HONEST!

If you can't do something, meet a deadline or be prepared in one way or another, let the requesting party know. It's better to tell someone from the beginning that you can—or cannot—do something. Follow-through is huge in this and every business. This, students, is another key aspect of business etiquette: don't say you can do the job unless you can!

Honesty goes a long way in my book. I'd rather someone be honest about their issues or challenges within a business scenario than try to present a different version of themselves. When this—a different version—is presented, I know I'll have to deal with BS down the line. Therefore, it's better for me to know what my realistic deliverables are so there are no disappointments.

FIND THE RIGHT COMMUNICATION CHANNEL!

There are different channels for different types of communication. For initial contact, or to send locations, etc., Facebook Messenger, Instagram, and other types of texts can work. For example, I will occasionally text basic details about a business opportunity or to see if someone is available. Then, I will email them the details to confirm.

Again, this is important for you all to know: for any business-relevant communication, it's important to use email. I'm talking about contracts and other business—these should go through email. And keep those documents! Email is technically a legal document and if a situation arises where you may have to go to court, you have records of the agreed-upon details.

And speaking of details, sometimes a simple phone conversation can also go a long way—and eliminate the need for tons of texts. Though I'm not a huge fan of the phone, I will hop on a call as a means of solidifying a relationship or business opportunity; there is still something to be said for hearing a person's tone of voice.

Finally, in the communication discussion, it's important to mention the need to listen. When you are on a business call, your first goal should be to listen first, and consider what you want to respond to or address prior to speaking.

Again—as far as communication is concerned, there are different modes for different objectives.

BE PREPARED!

In addition to determining which communication channel to use and when, you also need to be prepared as far as your attire, your bio, your CV, and your headshot. All these elements should complement each other—and help to define you as YOU!

Attire

Someone told me many years ago that people will see you before they hear you, and I'm sharing this with you here. Let me clarify first: I am not saying you need to wear name-brand clothing; I'm saying that you need to make sure that you are presentable and dressed for the occasion. The goal is to be appropriate. You don't ever want to stick out for not wearing the standard or code of what everyone else is wearing.

What is acceptable for business meetings?

For men: a suit or pressed pants with a sports coat, socks, and shoes—and I might add, it's nice to also get those shoes shined every now and then!

For women: a dress, skirt, or business suit with "sensible" shoes.

For both, be aware of how loose or tight your clothes fit, and head to the more conservative side of dress. Part of this quick judgment that people do of you relates to not only what you are wearing, but your style of dress. Too big or too tight sends a message that you might not want to send.

I have to tell you two tales here:

First, I noticed that after several of my female friends worked with and went on tour with Beyoncé, their sense of style and fashion went to a whole new level; they began to put great thought and effort into understanding and discovering their own personal style.

As far as my own experience in this area, I remember when we first started working with the Christian McBride Trio. Christian Sands and I were so thrilled to be working with McBride that we started wearing suits to the gigs because it was a big deal to us to play with him. At first McBride would laugh at us and tell us we didn't have to, but then he enjoyed it, and he started wearing suits again as well. Then we started to become known as a sharp dressing trio, which made audiences love to see us even more. Actually, dressing smartly is really a nod to our forefathers and mothers in music. They always dressed the part.

Bio (short and long)

Dressing well is not only part of what gives a first impression; your bio also says a lot about you and your level of professionalism, and this brings me to my next point. One of the key business essentials for advancement is a bio. Now stay with me—I'll talk about the résumé/CV in a moment. But first, the bio: a bio is a summary about you. It should be brief and concise—but complete. It should tell your story, including how you became interested in your craft, where you were formally trained, and the various relationships that can vouch for your experience and talent. Look at examples of bios of people within the field—especially those who are similarly talented or beyond where you currently are.

You'll want to have two versions: a short and a long. The short—perfect in program notes—can be between thirty-five and fifty words, while the long can be between seventy-five and 150. Obviously, it depends on the publication/audience, but you should always have both on hand, and in both Word and PDF formats.

Additionally, as in the case of any writing that will represent you, find a proofreader or writer who can assist you.

Résumé/CV

A résumé is a more than just a chronological list of your accomplishments and experiments; it's something that potential employers look at when they're trying to determine if you're the right one for the job. One search online will provide you with a number of examples. Keep your résumé neat, accurate, free of spelling errors, and up to date. A CV, or Curriculum Vitae, also shows your work experiences, accomplishments, and usually a bit of your pedagogical practices within your career résumé. The CV is mostly used in the States when applying for various academic positions. Again, make sure it's up to date.

Headshot

Just as in the case of dressing the part, and having well-written bios and résumés/CVs, your headshot is very important. I've met several musicians who initially thought that since they weren't actors, they didn't have to worry about the quality of their photos; this, dear student, is not the case. You should be prepared to represent yourself with a high-quality image of you. I recommend either a professional photographer or, if you can't afford a professional photographer, a photography student who knows about headshots.

As a performing artist, it will also be helpful to have performance shots as well. Make sure you are well-dressed in those photos. After all, having excellent-quality photos—just as in the case of the other materials I'm recommending you have—can make the difference between getting a gig and not.

Reflections for thought and discussion:

1. What basic business fundamentals do you already practice?
2. Do your current behaviors include the business etiquette tips mentioned here?

3. What is your preferred communication channel, and how does it match up with the tips given here?
4. Are you prepared with bios, a résumé, and a headshot?
5. Do you have someone you can ask to proofread your writing?
6. Do you have audition/interview-ready clothing?

Reflections for writing:

1. What basic fundamentals in business do you need to work on?
2. Write—off the top of your head—a short bio for yourself in less than fifty words.

CHAPTER 4

Business Planning and Navigation for Musicians

"Success usually comes to those who are too busy to be looking for it."—Henry David Thoreau, Essayist, Poet, and Philosopher

One of the challenges I had in school was that I wasn't educated as far as money, financial planning, and how both work with my being an artist. I was not prepared as far as creating a budget and a plan; these are key. So, when I first sat down with record producer and fellow Juilliard School professor Greg Knowles to tell him about my recording, the first thing he asked was for me to email him my pre-production plan, which would include my budget, timeline, and how I was going to complete this project. I was completely unprepared!

But then, I learned how to complete it all.

This section focuses on two key aspects of business planning. It focuses not only the creation of an individual's business plan, but also on the key relationship building that is an intrinsic part of creating any business. This section also includes tips for maintaining and growing these connections.

Before we even get started with this first part, let's talk a bit about what a business plan means for you. A business plan is essentially an outline of your goals, as well as the practical steps you need to take in order to achieve them, as well as the resources that you need. The business plan will help you—and the readers—grasp the scope and depth of a project, as well as the budget and the timeline.

Learning how to articulate your business plan will not only get someone interested in the idea of working with you, it will also help you to clarify what it is you want to do. Writing down your business plan helps you—and those you will present it to—to be able to examine the validity of a plan.

PART 1: HOW TO WRITE A BUSINESS PLAN

When I was growing up, my mom and grandmother used to quote a phrase to support their belief that I should write it all down. The phrase, which was somewhat loosely translated from the Bible, was, "Write the vision, make it plain, and at the appointed time it will come to pass." It was their way of saying: write it down and it will become real!

Well, dear students, I pass this wisdom along to you.

Here are some general steps for setting up a business plan and how to create your rough draft. As you'll see, I'm referring primarily to content—the meat of your plan—and to getting you started. After all, you want this to be as compelling to a reader as it is to you.

Of course, formatting is also key; a business plan not only has to sound good, it must look good! When you're ready, one search on the Internet will yield you many templates. But I wanted you to get the components of a business plan, and that's what I'm addressing in this first section. Also note: though I've addressed these components separately, they are going to be woven together and, just like in a great piece of music, work in different ways—maybe in different orders—to form a whole.

COMPONENTS OF A BUSINESS PLAN
The main business idea:
What is the "title" of your plan?

This is an easy question to ask, and may be hard to answer. But you can do it. Start by just getting all your business-related ideas down on paper. Focus first on the ideas—not the goals nor the end result. Then, once you've gotten everything "out," you can start to organize. This organization, by the way, can come hours, days, or even weeks later, once you've had time to really consider what it is you want to do. Then you can think about what the "title" or name of your business idea is. At this point, part of determining your main idea may be meeting with someone who works in the industry, and who can help you clarify your ideas and better put into words some of what you'd like to do.

The Objective—What is your overarching goal for this business?

Once you've determined your main business idea, the next step is to identify what you want to achieve. After all, you've thought about this—even in just coming up with the main idea of your business. Setting your goal—your objective—encompasses what you want to accomplish with your business idea.

The Team—Whom are you going to work with?

Something I learned early on: if you want to be successful, you NEED a team. No one is an island, and many of you reading this book probably have incredibly lucrative ideas. But perhaps what is lacking is the fact that you won't allow yourself to create the right team, or a team at all. If you feel this way, you're not alone: most people might think they don't want a team because maybe they want to avoid responsibility or accountability to others. Let's see if I can convince you otherwise of the importance of having a team.

One of the key things that I learned very early on in my career was analyzing what I was good at, and what I was *not* good at. When I am not good at something, I simply try to find the person who is the best at it, and work with him or her—so that I can get better. Alternatively, I let that person manage that area of the project. In doing so, I allow myself the opportunity to focus on what I am great at. Additionally, if you have experts all around, the project will be that much smoother, and ultimately, more successful in both execution and sustainability. Look around: every great business has a solid team behind it. Sustaining a project or a business only occurs with a great team. So, again, think about people who complement you, as well as those you complement.

Plan of Action—What are the steps you need to take to reach your goal?

This is where you list the steps of what is necessary to get moving, and get the doors open, or start increasing your profile, making your scores available, creating a demo—whatever is needed in order to make your objective a reality. A timeline of what it takes for you to fulfill these steps is a must. A timeline details realistic dates that coincide with your goals, as well as a course of action that will lead you to your objectives. This, your timeline, is going to help you to make sense out of your dream, and place structure around it so it can become a reality.

One way to build a cohesive timeline is to work backwards. Start by setting an end date. So, for example, you could say, "I want this album to be released by August 1." Then, ask yourself: What steps to I need to get there by then? Outline the concrete steps that it will take to achieve that goal in that time frame. Look at your calendar and start planning. Keep in mind, however, that sometimes you will run into delays, so you'll need to keep an element of flexibility in your planning. I always suggest building in the possibility of time delays.

Financials: Funding and Budget—Where is the money going to come from? How are you going to spend it?

This is a chance to really look at where the dollars and cents are potentially coming from, where they are going, and what exactly these funds will be applied to. Think about startup and operational costs. Do extensive research and be realistic, ideally without getting too overwhelmed; remember, this is all part of the process. In doing so, you can create a business plan with "real" numbers represented. Then you will have not only an idea of what your plan encompasses financially, but additionally, a potential funder will be also be able to assess your ability to understand the real costs required to attain your goal.

Your budget goes hand in hand with your whole financial process—and it can also determine your timeline. A budget is a document that details line items of what you are trying to do and what it will cost. Even before you start calling musicians into the studio, you need to create that budget: you need to understand how much money you have, and how to itemize and designate that money for the project completion. Now, students, I'm telling you all this because it must be on your radar—but you don't need to create a budget from scratch, and you certainly don't have to do this alone. As far as the creation goes, there are many budget templates, and you can definitely use what is comfortable for you. And note that it may even be worth hiring a producer or financial manager who can handle that portion of the project if you struggle. There are tons of financial managers out there, and you can also consider your friends who may not be artistic, but are great with handling money and numbers. Ask them for help!

I remember when I first started my production company, I was so interested in credits on my production résumé that I would go into full pre-production mode and rehearsals without knowing if the money was all there. Consequently, I ran into major delays—and big frustrations—because the plan was not in tandem with the budget. Though I learned invaluable lessons through this experience, I don't recommend this method at all. In fact, I suggest the contrary: do not start a project without the budget being considered. You don't want to start securing people's time, not to mention studios, etc., if there is no guarantee of where the money might be coming from.

And, speaking of people's time, this leads me into the next very important part of a Musician's Business Planning: relationships.

PART 2: CULTIVATING RELATIONSHIPS IN THE MUSIC BUSINESS

"I don't have problems, I have friends."—Clarence Alexander Avant, Music Executive, Entrepreneur, and Film Producer

The ability to create, manage, and sustain the right relationships is really the key to success in any business. Building your career involves an understanding of constructing and sustaining relationships. Relationships are the glue that hold businesses together globally; they are the bridges of connectivity, no matter how small or massive the company structure, from the very foundation up to the boardroom. People will be much more inclined to do business with you and help you when there is that connection.

I find that many people make relationships too transactional, and that is often why it's challenging for them to find success in the midst of their endeavors. Also, as artists, we sometimes feel that we can just be artistic and not adapt to the standard rules of engagement in terms of how we do business. There is also often an ignorance in thinking that relationships don't matter, and that talent is supreme. Well, dear students, that's not always the case, especially if you want to sustain your career over time. Someone will hire someone they know before hiring someone they don't—even if the latter is said to be more talented. As an artist, you must figure out how to build relationships around your art to support and sustain you. Otherwise, your road to "success" will be an incredibly challenging and isolated one.

In this section, I will define different types of relationships, and then give you tips for cultivating—and sustaining them.

Various types of relationships

While writing this book, I realized that I should clarify the various types of relationships that can be created and that you may encounter as a musician and artist. This is not a complete list—but it's a starting point for your consideration and reflection:

- Teacher to student
- Student to student
- Artist to manager
- Artist to booking agent
- Artist to PR agent
- Artist to artist

- Artist to producer
- Mentor to mentee
- Mentor to artist
- Artist to venue
- Artist to arranger
- Artist to fan
- Artist to promoter
- Artist to publicist
- Artist to brand manager
- Artist to accountant
- Artist to tour manager

THE ART OF BUILDING A BUSINESS RELATIONSHIP

How does one start a business relationship?

This may seem obvious, but this is a question that I get often when I am lecturing and teaching. Here are the tips I share with them, and now with you:

Always be genuine!

People respond to genuine energy, because it's just an enjoyment to be around someone who is authentic. I find that the more successful you become, the more people will feel they have to posture themselves in a certain way to be near you. With all of the famous and influential people that I have been fortunate to encounter in my life, I've found that being authentic and kind reaches everyone and unites them. From kings to queens, from celebrities to brilliant minds, everyone will positively respond to kindness and you showing up as your authentic self. Be interested, and listen. All you have to do is care. When someone senses your genuine care, they will unlock a whole world to you.

Understand your current position with that person!

As a student, be a student; don't try to make that person think that you are further along in your career to gain their interest. Yes, this is part of being genuine and being honest. When you try to be a peer and you aren't a peer, it shows lack of self-awareness. People can work with where you honestly are in your career. There are many times students reach out to me and ask me if we can go and grab coffee, and I am letting you know now: if you are not my friend, advisor, mentor or someone dear to me, I will not be grabbing coffee with you. That's something that's incredibly intimate for me, and reserved for people that I have close relationships with in my life. However, as a student, feel free to ask me for a lesson, or be honest and say what you really want. I find that many people make this mistake in seeking to get to close to someone without a real connection. Use your instinct and respect people's space and know what your position is currently in their lives. I get so many emails from musicians *that I don't even know*, asking me for things. When you start a relationship by giving, then you stand out in the crowd.

Build relationships in your formative years!

This bit requires some history—so stay with me here:

Within the Jazz Department at Juilliard, the Business of Music Professor was great, yet his focus (with his admittance) was on an antiquated record-label model that was being shattered by the invention of the iPod, shift in CD sales, and the emergence of streaming services like Apple Music and Spotify. Our first day in class, he asked, "What if Tower Records didn't exist anymore?" We all thought he was the "Musical Antichrist," but within a year, Tower Records on 66th Street—which we all loved—went out of business, and all the other locations in NYC closed within a year later.

With this reality, the idea of getting a record deal for my peers and me changed drastically. As a drummer, I was going to have to figure out a way to record my music, fund it, and release it all on my own. Keep in mind, students, that at this point, there were no "career-building sections" in our classes.

Now, stay with me here—this was when I got really resourceful. That same music business professor in the jazz division is an award-winning record producer. I went to him after I graduated and I told him about what I wanted to do. At that point I had already planned my recording, selected the studio, the band, tunes, etc. but I felt within that I needed some assistance.

That professor, Greg Knowles, came to my rescue. Now, here, I am back to my key point: the reason that he was so helpful—or part of the reason—was because I always had a great relationship with him while in college. And I was prepared and genuine when I went back to ask him for help. Subsequently, he not only assisted me with the process of making my first record, but also taught me about that process. He encouraged me, too; he was the first person to tell me that I had the potential to be a producer. He felt I had "big musical ears" beyond just being a sideman, and that opened a whole new world for me. Again—this was a relationship I started in school and cultivated. I encourage you to do the same.

Maintain the contact and follow up!

As that example illustrates, it's so important to keep in touch with people that you meet in school—especially professors and your music mentors that you connect with. As a teacher, I strive to do the same. I always tell students when I am at lectures, "Here is my email address, and anyone that writes me and stays in contact with me, I will help."

In a class of fifty students, about ten to fifteen will get the email address, and five or six will email me and follow up, and within a month, I won't hear from any of them again.

Know that if someone does give you an email address, that person is willing to build and maintain a relationship, and you can count on that person as a resource. Don't miss out on that opportunity.

Have knowledge about whom you want to connect with!

I had prayed for years to meet three people: Rickey Minor, Steve Jordan, and Quincy Jones. I have met all of them, and two of them are my mentors. But here I'm sharing the story of how I met Rickey.

My family and I were vacationing in California, and I was invited to the *Tonight Show* hosted by Jay Leno. Teddy Campbell invited us to see the show thanks to the connection of our mutual friend, Otis Brown III.

After the show, Teddy graciously introduced us to the band, and we met Rickey, whom I had been wanting to meet for years. When I shook his hand, I began to tell him how much I admired him and his work ethic, and I was just losing my mind because of how excited I was. My sister then stepped in, and also told Rickey about how much she enjoyed him on certain Whitney Houston performances in the nineties on several award shows. Well, that was it: Rickey looked at us, smiled, and said, "Teddy, I got them from here."

Rickey then took my family and me into his office and began to show us rare videos of Whitney Houston, and explained his process for building her shows. After that, he walked us to our car, and he told me that if I ever needed anything to call him or email him, and to stay in touch, especially when I was in Los Angeles. That relationship has been maintained now for many years.

In conclusion, when you are knowledgeable about who you are meeting and who you desire to create a relationship with, it changes the narrative and the person could possible unveil more of themselves to you. Don't just go in blind when you meet people; do your homework and be knowledgeable about them.

Be aware that your actions have reactions!

As stated before, everything you will ever need will come from relationships, paired with the ability to manage the right relationships. This goes beyond your talent and musical gifts. Especially in the realm of music, as a sideman, you are constantly walking into "new" rooms with combinations of people you haven't previously interacted with yet; instead of having the benefit of growing a relationship with your peers, you will often be thrown into one. A golden nugget here, dear students, is to recognize that the key to the success of a gig is chemistry, which means that not only do you need to get along, but also realize that personalities that do clash will not be invited back into the room. I learned this lesson when I was in college, and am sharing that story with you now.

When I was a young student, I was very clear about what I thought I needed to work on.

So, when a professor of mine suggested what I should be working on, I took offense. After all, I had been taught humility by my family and I well knew what I had to work on as far as my playing. Additionally, I wasn't used to a teacher who was so directive. My previous teachers asked me what I thought I should work on; they always asked my opinion. Therefore, when this professor clearly demonstrated that he wanted to be the person to tell me what I needed, we clashed.

Unfortunately, even over time, we didn't bond. I did not acquiesce, and wouldn't let him tell me what I needed. I was not interested in his style of teaching me when, as I saw it, I fully recognized what I need to learn.

At the same time, I was approached by a very famous jazz musician who was interested in my work. And, in the typical style of jazz musician hiring, he invited me to play at his home so that he could then decide whether to hire me for a gig. I was thrilled. I returned his call, and awaited the official call with the date and time of my "audition" session with him.

However, that call didn't come. Instead, during that same week, the professor with whom I was at odds with announced, "I know some of you are getting calls to play with people, but you don't even have an idea how connected this world is. Be cautious about your attitude and behavior in the classroom, because it can affect your life outside of the classroom."

Now let me say this, despite the situation I described, ultimately, my former professor and I resolved our differences. As he taught me, and I learned, it's a small and very connected world. We must properly manage our relationships in this business, because we don't know who is connected and to whom.

At this point, and with the acknowledgment that we are all human, there are times when, unfortunately, we make mistakes like behaving in a way that is detrimental to a relationship that we have.

The difference lies, however, in how you can learn from your mistakes, and not repeat the behavior that led to them.

HOW DO YOU BURN A BRIDGE?

Let's step back for a moment, and dive a bit deeper into what may constitute burning a bridge in the music industry:

- Speaking negatively about someone.
- Going back on your word, or what you promised.
- Double-booking yourself without proper communication and not having a replacement for the job.
- Not respecting someone's boundaries.
- Asking for an amount of money for the job that the employer finds offensive.
- Having a disagreement and not resolving it fully.

This is not a complete list; there are other ways to burn a job or connection, and most of them revolve around lacking integrity, honesty, consistency, and commitment.

It's very difficult to repair a bridge once it's been burned, so it's really important to manage relationships in the right way initially, so you don't have to go through the hard work of rebuilding and repairing.

HOW DO YOU REPAIR A BURNED BRIDGE?

You can repair a bridge with authentic kindness, care, and with time.

I am generally a nice guy, and I try to really stay consistent to my core values, which guard and protect me, but I have definitely made mistakes within certain business relationships. However, I have tried, as I suggest, to learn from these mistakes and, dear students, I share my knowledge with you here.

My best method for repairing relationships is to apologize genuinely. When you make a mistake, the key is to understand what part you played in those mistakes, and honestly, once you really acknowledge where you made the mistake and you communicate that with the other person, even if they don't want to enter into a relationship with you again, they'll respect you.

This being said, I do want to add that we don't get to choose if people want to forgive us or not. I understand that in this life, everyone handles hurt and pain differently, and sometimes even people who love you the most may have to distance themselves from you because of that love. It's important to just give people space to handle things the way they desire and accept their method.

Let's go back to the relationship I described previously, the fractured relationship with the professor I mentioned earlier. Years later, when I understood the core of how and why I made the mistake, I wrote him a sincere letter of apology. He subsequently wrote me back, in a note that moved me to tears, and told me that he was honored to see my growth, and forgave me for the actions of my past.

Now, I also realize I was lucky to get such a response, and I confess that I didn't write the note with that expectation. Of course, dear students, some people won't forgive you, but if you do burn a bridge and want to remedy the situation, do apologize. And, regardless of the response, you'll need—of course—to move forward. But a reconciliation attempt will make you that much stronger.

ALWAYS DO YOUR JOB WITH EXCELLENCE!

"If you care about anything you do, you will do it through excellence."—Dan Kariv, CEO of Multiple Companies, Inspirational Speaker

One of the qualities that I realized I had to become more intentional about was excellence. I started incorporating excellence into every facet of my work, life, and everything in between. Excellence is making that choice to give your absolute best in everything, dotting every i, and crossing every t, and not stopping until the idea and assignment is completed.

When I began the work that I do with my children at Don't Miss a Beat, my family's foundation, I realized that what I loved most about our familial commitment was that we operated with distinction in the realm of serving and teaching children. We have always done the best that we can while keeping the well-being of our children first and foremost in our consideration and decisions. What I recognize as a result is that this—our excellence and our constant striving for it—really affects them; it inspires them to reach higher in their own lives.

I only like to collaborate with people who truly work with excellence, because those who work that way will do whatever it takes to make sure the work is great.

Here's what I mean by excellence:

Keep and maintain your work ethic

Much of my motivation shifted a few years ago, because I started understanding that everything I wanted to accomplish was on the other side of me re-tooling my work ethic. What I mean is that I saw that it wasn't a matter of what was available to me or not. If I could muster up the strength to work hard, in time, success could be mine in whatever area I was pursuing. I also heard the great Warren Buffett say, "Someone can be smarter than you, but not more disciplined." What does this mean? Working hard is fundamental.

I remember early in my college career, Victor Goines, who was the Artistic Director at Juilliard, really challenged me and called me out. He said that I was really talented, but a little lazy. I resented that comment, and channeled it into inspiration: that day, I pledged to myself that no one would ever be able to say that about me.

Even today, I have held on to that promise. In fact, people often say to me, "Man, you work so hard! You need to slow down!" I much prefer hearing this—and I guarantee and promise you that none of what you actually want to happen in your life will happen if you don't maintain your work ethic. Work hard—and consistently!

Another part of having a strong ethic is learning when to say yes, and conversely, when to say no. As a hardworking artist, we want to be constantly wanted—and affirmed for our talent. Constantly being in demand is something that feeds our ego and gives us confidence to keep going. However, if we want to maintain the quality of what we do, we must learn to be thoughtful about what we do and not say yes to all. Make your yes—and your no—powerful and in line with your work ethic.

Manage your time well

Part of maintaining your work ethic relates to what I was just saying about being thoughtful about what you do and don't do: it's learning to manage your time well.

This has been the key to my life in the last few years when the workload has tremendously increased. There was a time when I would be in one city for several months without traveling. Now, when I am in a city for ten days, that feels like a month to me. I have had to learn to accomplish in one day what takes some a week. Don't get me wrong; I love to sleep in, but now I have to wake up every day at a certain time, because if I don't, my work will snowball. Additionally, I now incorporate exercise into my day, so my body is in shape and ready for the rigorous schedule. I have also become way more strict about how I spend my time because I simply don't have a lot of it.

Once I started representing and working in the aspect of an artistic director and more leadership positions, I realized that being *ahead* of time is literally the only way I survive. My life is full of busy and non-busy moments. I've learned that now I can always sense the non-busy moments and manage my time to take full advantage of them. I am very diligent about knowing what my workload is, staying tuned into it, and working on a little bit every day. Know that I don't work on everything every day; I prioritize and set my schedule accordingly.

You can start now! Get yourself a calendar if you don't have one, or use your phone and start plugging those commitments in. Have a look, and prioritize. Yes, things will always come up, but if you have it noted, you'll be able to deal with it. Additionally, respond to calls/emails in a timely manner; don't let them linger.

Highly acclaimed jazz bassist Ben Wolfe told me years ago while I was in college that I would never have more time to perfect my craft than at that point in my life. I share this with you, dear students: the minute you graduate, your mind will have to be split between what you love and what you have to do to survive. This is where time management plays a huge and crucial role. I encourage you to NOT wait until you graduate; take time management into consideration now!

Find at least one mentor!

Speaking of considerations, one of the keys to your success as a musician will be mentorships.

These mentorships are the most powerful relationships that an aspiring artist can have. Mentors are essentially people who open up the pages of their lives to allow you read and benefit, as you are writing your own story. Mentors are also those who have walked a similar path to the one you are you are taking, and can give you the right kind of advice to anchor and equip you for your journey. Having the right mentor at each stage of your life and career can guide you in countless ways.

In my case, I've been fortunate to have different mentors for and at different stages of my professional life. I urge you to seek out the same.

Here's the story of my top three mentors:

One of the first major mentors that I remember having was my cousin, Kevin Sibley. Kevin, a talented actor and musician in New York City, fed and piqued my curiosity as a musician. In addition to inviting me to spend a lot of time with him and his college musical friends and bandmates, Kevin constantly brought home cassette tapes of jazz records. Additionally, he was the one to take me to see and hear Wynton Marsalis live in Fernandina Beach, Florida—an event that altered the entire direction of my life.

Mulgrew Miller was the second impactful mentor who entered my life. A great husband, father, and mentor to many young musicians, he dispelled the myth that to be a great musician, you had to have a dysfunctional life. Mulgrew taught me the reality of a jazz musician, as someone who lives with integrity, honesty, and humility.

Today I am exceptionally grateful to my mentor and friend Alexander Smalls, who has shown me what it is to be an entrepreneur, author, and paradigm shifter. Alexander is someone who lives life on his own terms and makes the world pull a chair to the table that he has set and prepared for them. In being who he is, he really allowed me to understand myself better, identify my blind spots, and seek to strengthen and better myself. He challenges me to always communicate with clarity and grace, which empowers me get through whatever challenges life brings. Alexander always encourages me to step into unknown territory and achieve more than I dream of, which is pretty hard to do because I am a big dreamer! He has also facilitated my cultivating key relationships for both my life and career. For example, because he was fully aware of what I desired to accomplish with this book, he connected Arlen to me so that we could collaborate. And finally, because of all he has done and continues to do for me, he was the perfect person to write the afterword for this book.

How can you find a mentor? Look around and find someone you want to be like. Understand that most people are crazy busy, but respect their time—and guide them into realizing you're worth the investment, while keeping realistic expectations. Again, your mentor/mentee relationships are like the ones we've been discussing, and they must be based on mutual respect and trust. Building one takes time; it needs time to grow. The key to establishing the right mentor-to-mentee relationships is, in my opinion, the ability to create win-win scenarios for all involved.

In conclusion, it's key for you to build a network around your life and career. Your network is your net worth—and this does not, dear students, relate simply to monetary gains. Being very wealthy and rich, with resources and people who are not only successful, but also whole and balanced, will be fruitful. As my friend Albert Rivera stated in one of our meetings, "Follow the human, and the money is after." Meaning that if you follow the instinct of being human, and caring for other humans, somewhere in that will be an opportunity to grow, which will allow for additional success.

Reflections for thought and discussion:

1. What are the key components of a business plan that you have already considered?

2. What are the components for a business plan that you haven't considered and how will you tackle them?

3. What does "cultivating relationships in the music business" mean to you?

4. What are you doing now to build business relationships?

5. Have you ever burned a relationship bridge? If so, did you repair it? If you haven't, how might you repair it?

6. What does having a work ethic mean to you?

7. How do you currently keep track of appointments and deadlines? How can you be more effective in this area?

Reflections for writing:

1. Write three ideas for businesses/business plans that you would be interested in developing.

2. Write down the name of one mentor you currently have— or would like to have—and write a short description of that person, as well as how you might be able to convince him or her to take you on as mentee.

3. What are the qualities this person has that you would most like to emulate?

PART II

THE MUSIC INDUSTRY

In Part I, I wrote that you needed to start thinking differently about the music business, and business plans, as well as cultivating relationships and the right way to expand and sustain your business. Well, dear students, part of that involves your being able to learn more about the industry itself so that you can effectively function within it. We've spoken about maximizing your environments, building your career profile, and what you need to know about business, as well as business planning. Here, I invite you to take a deeper dive into this world to help you with the consideration of the broad range of roles within the music industry. I'm also—in this section—providing you with the tools for navigation as far as personnel and their responsibilities, relevant deals, and the importance of interactions with companies and representation.

CHAPTER 5

The Roles Within the Music Industry

It's our job as musicians to know the roles within the music industry, and be informed about who is necessary and when. The goal is that you succeed—and also that you protect yourself. Have you heard stories of talented people being ripped off because they fell for a "promised success" scheme? As you may recognize, being talented is not enough. You need to be smart, and music-business savvy, too.

I remember teaching about these roles in a class, and I remember the students saying to me how shocked they were to realize how many opportunities there were beyond performing and composing in the music business. In fact, it takes many roles and disciplines to keep the music business going. Additionally, in our new age of technology and social media, because of the new pathways music is moving into, the roles are increasing.

The following are mainly positions that you will encounter at some point as creatives within the business of music. This list is not complete, but it will help you shape a role you might reach for as you look/ explore your best fit, which may, of course, change over time.

ROLES
A&R Director

The artist and repertoire (A&R) director is typically the position that is responsible for finding and signing talent. When you check out documentaries about musicians, and their journey towards success, you'll note that an A&R director was involved somewhere in the process.

Accountant

An accountant for artists and music businesses plays an essential role in the business aspect of any musician. This is the person that helps musicians and music-industry professionals with a myriad of money related issues: bookkeeping, generating profit and loss statements, creating budgets for business plans, managing taxes, assisting with financing applications, analysis of contracts, business plans, and pretty much everything concerning financial management and planning.

Agent

An agent or booking agent is a person that acquires work for an artist or group. This is the person that negotiates fees and is the intermediary between the venue, promoter, and artist.

Arranger

A musical arranger is a person or entity that makes a living re-arranging compositions and arrangements for various ensembles like orchestras, bands, vocalists, and even schools. Especially on Broadway, this person can make a great deal of money due to the necessity of taking music originally composed for one entity, and altering it for a different ensemble size.

Assistant

This person can work either independently with an artist or for a major executive within a record label, booking agency, management company, or other business entity. The assistant typically gets the grunt work done.

Attorney (Entertainment)

Within the music business, an entertainment lawyer is typically who creatives will want to hire to sort out contracts, record deals, business agreements, and establish business entities like LLCs or set up company structures.

Background Vocalist

This is a vocalist who primarily makes a living being the support behind a lead vocalist on tour, or else in the studio.

Club Promoter

This person works for a music club and handles booking bands and artists primarily for that club, or a group of clubs.

Composer

This person composes and and often directs original music either for orchestra, television, film, bands, video games, and any other type of media entertainment. Composers have a great ear for music, and are often skilled in playing one or several instruments.

Educator

This title can extend into many realms, ranging from private music teacher to a professorship, and including the position of music teacher at a school and/or musical academy.

Music Contractor

A music contractor is the person who contracts musicians for orchestras, Off-Broadway and Broadway shows, film scores, and virtually any major musical opportunity, especially when dealing with union halls and theaters.

Music Director

A music director is typically a person who is not only a musician, but also the leader of a production, band, tour, or recording. Some music directors operate in various capacities; depending on the scale of the production, they may be very hands-on with the musician. Other music directors may operate more like administrators or concept-creators. In this case, they may hire an assistant music director to handle the musical element of a show or project.

Music Distributor

Though aspects of the music distributor's role is evolving, the general idea remains the same: they are typically responsible for linking an independent musical group—or a label—to consumers. They often oversee the marketing, promotion, and distribution of a group's CDs/LPs to retail outlets. In the same way, they distribute via online outlets and work with the tons of digital companies globally to get your music out there.

Personal Manager

A manager is a person that manages a professional musician's career and life, kind of like a career architect. A manager creates the right strategy for the goals a musician may have in mind. A manager also works closely with a booking agent to make sure that the work and goals are complementing each other, and will lift the musician to the next level of success.

Producer

A music producer is a person who is integral in creating an album for an artist or group. Though there are many versions of what a producer is or should be, basically, the producer is the person who knows who needs to be in the room—and when. That person also has the key role of facilitating a musical vision and seeing it through until completion. I personally prefer music producers who are musicians, not beat makers.

Publicist

A publicist is the person in charge of marketing, or assembling a PR team for a project or album. Publicists coordinate with the record label, management, and the talent's agency to maximize the promotional side of the musician's career.

Publisher

Music publishers are companies that make sure the musicians get paid for the royalties and rights associated with their songs. I work with ASCAP, and I have friends that work with SESAC and BMI, who are also very reputable companies. Some musicians even have created their own publishing companies, and partner with larger publishing entities.

Recording Artist

A recording artist is a musician who records music and/or musician who makes money by selling audio recordings.

Recording Engineer

A recording engineer a person who records music typically at a studio, or occasionally on site at a venue for a special project. This individual is of paramount importance when you start to record your own catalogue of music or with other musicians. The right recording engineer makes everything wonderful, and, conversely, the wrong one wastes time and money. In my case, when I am producing sessions, I have a very short list of engineers I like to work with.

Sideman/Sideperson

A sideman or sideperson makes a living performing, touring, and recording with various artists as part of their bands and bringing their musical vision to life.

ADDITIONAL ROLES

Downbeat Magazine, in their October 2019 issue, published a great article entitled "50 Great Jobs for Musicians," written by James Hale and Bobby Reed. They listed some additional roles that I think are important to include as part of this ever-evolving music industry.

Artist Liaison/Administrator for City/County/State

Various state fund granters and organizations need people to assist in activities related to artists and special events.

Commercial Music Composer

This composer specifically creates music for TV shows, commercials, and movies.

Hospitality Coordinator

This person handles catering and beverage support for festivals and venues, and ensures that the artists are taken care of prior to, during, and after a show.

Instrument Technician

Many high-profile artists employ guitar, drum, keyboard, and audio-visual technicians to accompany and support the tour.

Music Festival Director

This is becoming an increasingly valued position as various festivals are looking for musician personalities to assist, direct, and give insight and guidance in booking and festival planning.

Music Instrument Marketing Specialist

Various musicians, if they are struggling within their freelance career, may pursue a position with a musical instrument manufacturing company. Due to the prevalence of social media, many companies are looking for musicians who can also work in the area of marketing. Due to the need for daily content creation to bring more exposure to the products, it's helpful to have musicians in this role.

Music Instrument Resale Specialist

This is a person that may assist with antique instruments, or work in tandem with an online company to re-sell instruments.

Music Store Staff

Due to online sales, the decline of music stores has become a reality. Still, there remain some local, regional, and national chains of music stores in existence and in need of knowledgeable staff.

Music Streaming Service Staff Member

The music industry now involves streaming, and many of the streaming companies (Spotify, Apple Music, Pandora, Google Play, etc.) have departments that hire staff to assist with this ever-growing arena.

Piano Tuner

Because venues, schools, universities, studios, festivals, clubs, and concert halls have pianos, and because they require tuning, being a piano tuner can be a lucrative career. After all, pianos need regular servicing. Additionally, many companies like to have the same piano tuner time after time, and will often keep the same one for years.

Recording Studio Manager (and Support Staff)

Musicians will always need to record music, and therefore recording engineers are always necessary. There are still quite a few studios that record locally, regionally, nationally, and internationally. This includes quite a few universities, colleges, and conservatories that have built their own state-of-the-art recording studios on campus, and need skilled managers and support staff to logistically run their studios.

Self-Employed Artist

Also known as a freelance artist, a self-employed artist is someone who is essentially employed by him or herself and works with various contractors, organizations, and companies.

Sound Technician (for Clubs and Concerts)

This person operates the sound for venues, which can be a full or part-time job, with daily commitments to the different venues.

Staff Publicist

A publicist is a person that handles all of the public relations for an artist. However, a staff publicist will handle media relations for the company or venue, as well as every artist and entity booked at or in association with the venue.

Subscriptions/Ticket Services Director

The role of a subscriptions or ticket services director position consists of handling all of the event ticketing, including dispensing on the day of a show, as well as advance ticket sales. In addition to event ticket sales, there are often a large number of donors and fans of the venue who will buy a subscription for the entire season, and so this same person would be very involved in responsibilities related to procuring these tickets as well. This position can also be a part- or full-time commitment.

Tour Manager

A tour manager's role can sometimes fall under the management's responsibilities. However, more specifically, a tour manager ensures the artist and all supporting parties for the band are taken care of. A tour manager assists with band setup, travel, booking flights, advancing concerts, assisting with transportation, and also occasionally running sound for events. In general, it's the tour manager's job to make sure the tour is successful. For this reason, this person must be flexible, adaptable, and have the ability to problem solve.

University Music Department Staff

Many universities, both in the States and elsewhere, have a music program. Thanks to these programs, there are various relevant positions. These include some of the positions on this list, but within the university sector. Because most universities function beyond the school year, this position can be a full-time one.

Venue/Concert Hall Manager

This person maintains the daily upkeep and staff maintenance of the venue. Additionally, this position may require certain computer skills, as well as the skill of dealing with various vendors. This can be a full-time job.

Venue/Concert Hall Marketing Director

Responsibilities for this role, like those of any marketing position, include making sure that the public is informed about what's happening at a venue. This position is normally a full-time position.

CREATE YOUR OWN ROLE

In conclusion, though I've listed many roles here, I want to add an additional thought: if there is a role that you desire to create within the industry that doesn't exist yet, do it. I have always been a huge advocate for trailblazing. In fact, one of the things that I embrace at this juncture of my career is forging new paths. As Mulgrew told me many years ago, "There is always room for another great musician in New York City." I encourage you to additionally consider that there is always room for a new role and path in the music industry.

And, to this end, I leave this chapter, dear students, with a relevant proverb: "Fortune favors the bold."

Reflections for thought and discussion:

1. What are roles have you played thus far in your experience as a musician? Describe your role, responsibilities, and what skills you needed to carry out that role.
2. What are roles that you have encountered? Explain the situations and the "players" of those roles. What skills did they have? Were they successful in these roles? Why or why not?
3. What roles were new to you?
4. Why might certain roles be relevant at certain times in your life? Explain with examples.
5. What does "Fortune favors the bold," mean to you?

Reflections for writing:

1. Write three roles from the list in this chapter that piqued your interest.

2. Now write down the skills needed to be successful at these roles.
3. Consider what you could do to attain these skills, and write down steps you would take to get there.

CHAPTER 6

The Deal with Deals

"Things ain't what they used to be. . . ."—Duke Ellington, Composer, Pianist, Leader of a Jazz Orchestra, with a music career that spanned more than six decades.

When I got accepted to Juilliard in April of 2001, my dream was that after I spent four years at my dream school, I'd immediately be signed to Blue Note Records, or Verve, and then begin my journey as a successful jazz musician, traveling the world with my band and selling records.

Of course, things don't always happen as planned. . . .

In August 2001, I moved to New York City. Three weeks later, September 11th happened. This altered—and ended—many lives. Then there was the subprime mortgage crisis.

After that, during my freshman year, the first edition of the iPod was released.

By the time I finished my education at Juilliard, the record business was no longer what I imagined it to be. A lot of the employers and people that I looked up to and admired, and even those that had been beneficiaries of these amazing contracts that I dreamed of, had been completely changed. The record labels could no longer support these contracts at large, and their opportunity for recoupment of their investment in various albums had been totally ruined.

Subsequently, everyone had to step back and create newer, more sustainable strategies.

Speaking of taking a step back, let's consider Duke Ellington's quote—but take a historical perspective. We're going to get some background before coming back to the present, and examining how to navigate music industry negotiations, or what I like to call today's deals—with deals.

PART A: HISTORY OF THE MUSIC RECORDING INDUSTRY—AND THE EFFECT ON TODAY'S RECORDING DEALS

This is important, dear students, so that you have a bit of a foundation and can trace why things are the way they are. Now stay with me here; this will help build your music business knowledge foundation.

The birth of copyright laws

According to F.M. Scherer from John F. Kennedy School of Government, Harvard University (October 2008) in, "The Emergence of Musical Copyright in Europe from 1709 to 1850," the first modern copyright law was the Statute of Anne, enacted in the United Kingdom in 1709. (It was so named because of its passage during the reign of Queen Anne.)

It was assumed at first that the law did not cover printed music. However, Johann Christian Bach, a.k.a. "London Bach," whose works were pirated by James Longman, filed a case in 1773, and the ruling ended up being in his favor. However, Bach gained nothing monetarily and he died a destitute man. Though Bach financially got the short end of the stick, others benefited greatly and began filing their copyrights under the Statute of Anne, and the registrations increased to over 1,828 copyrights filed in the 1790s. In 1842, musical performances were added to the Statute of Anne, to protect artists. Following the French revolution, the United States passed a copyright law in 1790, and added performance rights in 1870.

However, in Germany, Austria, Czechoslovakia, and northern Italy, things were quite different. In 1829, Austrian music publishers entered a new anti-piracy agreement and set up a central registry to communicate who had exclusive rights to which works. The first person to benefit in a major way from this arrangement was Italian-born operatic composer Giuseppe Verdi. Verdi's publisher and business manager, Giovanni Ricordi, whose publishing firm is still in existence today, was apparently an economic genius. He saw the full potential of what copyright opportunities were available and fully exploited them. He put a halt to the distribution of Verdi's scores that were being procured from his copyists to mount his operas in various opera houses in Italy. Instead the local opera impresarios were required to use official Ricordi scores and pay performance fees. Also, for smaller houses, and places that could not perform the larger version of the production, he had Verdi's assistants prepare "reductions"—scores for individual arias, and overtures from each opera for voice with piano, solo piano, four hands piano, voice with violin, small ensembles, and more. The demand from opera houses that wanted the full score was limited to a few dozen theatres. However, thanks to those numerous houses that purchased the reduction scores, Ricordi's company made a ton of money, and they became very rich—as did the composer. As a result of Verdi's financial success, he wrote fewer operas with each coming decade. This, writing less but earning more, became a trend of other great operatic composers like Rossini and Donizetti.

The birth of the recording industry and the record label

The first phonograph-type instrument is said to be the paleophone, an invention from Charles Cros. Though no trace of a working paleophone was ever found, Cros is remembered as the earliest inventor of a sound recording and reproduction machine. After that, the first practical sound recording and reproduction device was the mechanical phonograph cylinder, invented by Thomas Edison in 1877 and patented in 1878.

In 1887, Emile Berliner invented the gramophone player and the flat disc phonograph records that it used, which played sound recorded on a flat record made of shellac, which took the place of Edison's cylinder. (These records, made of natural shellac, would later be replaced in the 1930s with synthetic resins.)

The very first phonograph company, called Edison Speaking Phonograph Company, was established in 1878. Twenty years later, after a lot of competition, including company purchases paired with legal battles, Edison's then-named National Phonograph Company ultimately dissolved. During that same time period, others sought the rights to start recording phonographs—and inventors came up with different variations and improvements.

In the late 1880s, commercially released phonograph records of musical performances became available. Later, in the 1920s, the onset of widespread radio broadcasting forever changed the way music was heard and listened to.

On February 25, 1925, Columbia Records—today's oldest surviving brand name in the recorded sound business, named after its DC birthplace—began involving the electric recording process licensed from Western Electric, which was the entry point into creating 78 rpm records.

From its inception, Columbia Records had several artists who they signed so that they could sell records. As recording technology increased, the ways with which they could produce music of all types expanded. It's important to note that at that point, and for many years to follow, the whole reason record companies existed was so that they could sell records. For this reason, though the basic model/template of a record company has evolved through the years, it has maintained the same focus: a record company exists to promote the technology of records and ultimately sell more.

Present-day recording

Fast forward to today: the amount of record companies that can still afford to be in business is dwindling drastically because technology has removed the mass demand for a physical product like 78s, LPs, cassettes, 8-tracks, and even CDs. Today the average consumer gets access to the music for free via streaming services like Spotify, Tidal,

Apple Music, Google Music, or Amazon Music and downloading MP3 files to their phone, tablets or laptops. So instead of the record company needing a product as the go-between, their product goes directly into people's phones and homes. Consequently, the way to fully monetize musical consumption to each individual has almost dissipated; music is practically free right now, and, as the years increase, it will be harder to fight that model. Obviously, a small niche market of audiophile lovers and vintage lovers are still buying LPs. In fact, according to a *Rolling Stone* September 2019 article, written by Elias Leight, "Vinyl Is Poised to Outsell CDS for the First Time Since 1986," it has been predicted that revenue from record sales may surpass the monies generated by the sale of CDs.

The important thing to think about recordings is that if you are a serious musician, and you plan on having any level of a career, you need to make a record. A recording is your calling card, and it allows the world to hear what you have to say musically, in addition to giving you a musical identity. Without a recording, or something with their "voice" in the airwaves, people are not considered legitimate artists. Even if you have to self-release and distribute, get something out there. This also a great way to start the journey that could eventually lead you to a recording contract. So many of my friends who have major deals right now have at least one or several albums they funded themselves first. Many of them are still financing their own records and just licensing them with major labels for distribution and PR deals. This means you pay for all of the initial costs to make the record, and the label makes sure a publicist is paid for three to four months to promote the record, and they distribute it to all of the digital outlets and few remaining physical stores domestically and internationally.

Again, my goal here—and with this whole book—is to give you a realistic look based on today's music business based on current facts with my own experiences. The goal is to equip you with the tools/insights that will be helpful for your own artistic journey.

I'm going to present a few realistic models that are in existence. I will tell you a little about my experiences both as a sideman and recording artist, and maybe it can give you some insight for your journey with labels. (Within the jazz market, we are still operating at about 1.0% in terms of consumption in comparison to the other genres. This is based on Nielsen US Music Mid-Year report which provides an exclusive glimpse at the music industry's leading trends, data, and trends from the latter part of 2019.)

PART B: TODAY'S RECORDING DEALS: WHAT ARE YOUR CRUCIAL CONSIDERATIONS?
Who is worthy of a recording deal?

It's important to first have a conversation about who is going to be appealing to labels. This is a big subject to me, one that has haunted me most of my career and caused a great deal of frustration and lamentation until I one day really looked at it from their perspective. This, dear students, is what I'm about to share with you.

Food for thought:

1. Record labels have to make money off of records.
2. Record labels need to make money off of records.
3. Record labels must make money off of records.

Make sense yet? The reason why I state this several times is because many artists, including me, get caught up in the grandeur of having a deal. The record deal is still great—it will, as I mentioned earlier, add a level of legitimacy to your career. However, what's worse is to get the deal and not satisfy the number of units that need to be sold for the company to make a profit from what they initially invested in you.

Consider these facts:

- Most labels are not making any money from CDs, and definitely not enough from streaming to justify the investment that they are making in their artists.
- Most labels, not excluding boutique labels, are looking for artists these days who have a following and can assist with a lot of the legwork of promoting themselves.

In other words, you have to show up already having it together in some way.

Let's take a look at my case:

My scenario was unique, because I have spent the last ten to fifteen years recording with high-profile artists who had track records, large audiences, and even previous recordings with these labels. In my case, I had relationships with these labels as a drummer, and even a reputation as a record producer, because many of the labels had signed artists that I had discovered as a result of producing their first records.

However, let me share this: when I initially stood before record labels as Ulysses Owens Jr., the bandleader and artist, they politely and quickly declined.

Of course, I was upset.

Still, I recognized that because I had not built a track record yet as an artist, I had not taken the time to build a following around my own personal brand of music. Consequently, I couldn't guarantee that I was going to move tons of units on my own name. Furthermore, I am a drummer, and in today's market it's very difficult for labels, even in jazz, to consider a drummer a legitimate and viable recording artist.

Conversely, those same labels would ask me to be part of a record with a lesser-known talent, because they could potentially sell more records. Why? Well, despite being the unknown talent, they fit into the profile that the label wanted to support. Frustrating for me? Most certainly.

So, what does this mean to you?

This means that you have to really be careful about how you enter the industry and how much time to dedicate with certain people, because once you build that artistic equity with fans, and supporters, many times they don't want you to change from how they fell in love with you—and you want to keep your audience happy!

Bottom line: With all that said, deals are not personal; they are deals. Assess your talent, your following, and your ability to create a product that people will buy.

Here's a scenario that might help you gain a good picture of the current state of the recording business: If someone gave you $20,000.00, and they said, "I want you go out and find an artist who is talented, and someone who you will invest in their record, PR, and touring. I need to see that $20,000.00 returned fully in profit six months after the release of their project."

I think you would choose artists completely differently if you were now entrusted with the same task.

Welcome to the recording business!

TYPES OF RECORDING DEALS

Now let's get down to deals:

I'm going to share my experiences with you, as well as information about my own experiences with recording deals.

In my case, I've had a few really unique opportunities to work with major labels like Sony, Universal/EMI, Mack Avenue, and Concord records, and these are the "Big Boys" of the record industry. They are all in: they are not only funding the albums, but also the ones who can lead you to be considered for Grammy Award nominations and potential wins.

If you are interested in being represented by a label, study the records they have released and the track record of artists they like to sign. If possible, speak to someone at the label, and ask them what they are looking for. This will give you an indication if you are, in fact, someone they would even consider. Just so you know, these days all labels are very much looking for whether you have buzz: Do you have a social media following? Do you have a pre-established audience that is ready to receive the product they are waiting for? At this point in time, labels cannot afford to take a big risk that will produce a major loss. For this reason, many of my friends who have a label deal in jazz are those who have the criteria just mentioned, or, for those a younger generation, have fortunately experienced some kind of competition win or opportunity for major exposure that makes the label feel like there is an audience waiting for them.

But let's go back a bit to other possibilities: there are a few different types of recording deals, and it's important to understand that not all deals are created equal, and not everyone will be offered the same kind of deal structure. Supply and demand still rule the recording business, and it's important to understand that the more you can leverage your own following and self-generating support system, the more you will be attractive to record labels. Again, you'll see that the key components I've mentioned—relationship building and persistence—will also play starring roles in this aspect of your career.

Self-released record

When I started recording my first album, I didn't have a visible profile at all. Despite the fact that I had done some touring with some major artists as a drummer, labels just weren't really interested in signing me. For this reason, I funded my first project, *It's Time For U*, with my own money. Between my savings, my partner at the time, and some relatives, we were able to put some funds together, but I had a bare-bones budget of $7,000.00, and was additionally lucky to have the support of my gracious friends. That album featured Ben Williams on bass (who had just moved to NYC), Sullivan Fortner on piano, Adam Burton on trumpet, Tim Green on alto saxophone, vocals of Alicia Olatuja, Danny and Eric Hall on trombone and saxophone, and yours truly. I self-released the album, and then just had a small digital distribution plan with Tunecore.com, a great company that will allow you to pay a small fee to get your music out in the major digital stores domestically and globally (using iTunes, Amazon Music, etc.) This whole experience was hugely helpful just to start the journey as a recording artist, and taught me much about the process of making a record.

Cash & carry record

This kind of deal—Cash & Carry Record—is a term I coined myself. What it means, essentially, is that the label gives you cash, and they carry the record. It's simple—and has no strings attached. They own your masters, and your publishing rights, and they give you and the band money to make the record.

In addition to teaching me about the process, the experience I just described previously also helped me focus on my goals—and next steps. Once *It's Time For U* was released, I not only realized that I wanted to make a record for a label, but also with an all-star cast of jazz luminaries. I started touring quite a bit with Christian McBride and Nicholas Payton, and the Christian McBride trio was starting to form and tour with McBride, Christian Sands, and me.

At that point, because McBride was still in the middle of promoting his quintet's album *Inside Straight*, thanks to stellar jazz label Mack Avenue Records, he had not made any plans yet to record the trio. So, I had the idea to record the trio first, as well as to make an album with the musicians I loved playing with so much. After all, we had a lot of potential together thanks to the combination of musical respect and our relationship and overall mentorship McBride provided to Christian Sands and me. In regard to my relationship with Nicholas Payton, I started working with him after being introduced via McBride's Big Band, and we instantly made a serious musical connection. He is, after all, one of the greatest musicians on the planet—and he created #BAM (hashtag Black American Music). On top of that, Nicholas and I had always loved Jaleel Shaw's playing. Additionally, tenor and bass trombonist (as well as composer and producer) Michael Dease had also been a really great friend and collaborator of mine, so I decided that he would also be on my second recording.

I started shopping the idea with various labels, and because I wasn't a high-profile leader, in their opinion, many of them weren't interested; they didn't see how I was going to pull this record off. I persisted, as I always do, and I believed in the power of my idea coming to fruition despite to the lack of faith I was encountering. I also considered raising money, but I felt that the concept and future recording were both good enough to be supported by a label, so I didn't give up. I kept brainstorming about what direction I should go.

And then, the dots started to connect. I remember being on tour in Amsterdam one evening and jazz bassist Reuben Rogers, whom I didn't know personally, was standing backstage with me. He asked me how I was doing, and then, to my delight, started telling me he was proud of the moves I was making. At that very moment, Gerry Teekens, the owner of Criss Cross records, which is based in Amsterdam, was standing next to me. So, Reuben addressed him.

"Hey man, meet this young cat, Ulysses Owens Jr.! You will be recording him soon! Y'all should connect!"

After that I encounter, I emailed Gerry about my album idea, and he loved the idea of the record. Gerry, known for being the label and guy that records the first albums of a lot of well-known jazz musicians, dug the idea and wanted to sign me. His was not a full-fledged recording deal. However, his deal did help me move forward.

Gerry basically gave me a flat fee, took care of recording and mixing costs, and did no promotion at all. That was honestly enough for me, because I didn't really have the extra income to record and also mix and master this record at that time. Gerry's plan took care of making this album happen.

Once the album was completed. I still needed some kind of promotion. I called my friend Kari Gaffney (Kari-On Productions) and asked her if we could create a limited PR campaign to get the music out there. We created a targeted campaign with very specific markets in mind. I have to tell you, Kari was amazing. As a result, I had physical distribution in the USA and Europe. It was this record that really put me on the radar with the press and the industry, in addition to my sideman work.

This is all to show you, dear students, that often there is more than one way to put the pieces of a puzzle together, but all the ways require persistence, faith, and—as I've told you before—a great team. I am really proud of the fact that this record actually happened, and it truly documented where I was at that moment in time. This tale, again, is included here to encourage you: if your idea is strong enough, and you maintain your relationships, there is a team out there that will help you bring your plans to fruition.

360 deal

A 360 recording deal is when a label signs you and they want money from everything that you do—your record sales and your tours—and they can also open doors. In other words, they take commission for all your work, but in return, you can reach audiences in a way that you can't necessarily do on your own.

Let me backtrack a bit to explain: for about five years, Japan became a very fortuitous market for my career and gave me an opportunity to form a partnership with a really great boutique record company called Spice of Life records. I met Tomoki Sassa through my friend and talented pianist and composer Takana Miyamoto, who had hired me to record a trio record with her and Matt Penman. I really loved the relationship she had with Sassa San, as I call him, and I had some ideas I wanted to share with him because I felt that he could facilitate the achievement of my recording goals in Japan. So Sassa and I had a long meeting one day when I was touring in Japan, and I spoke to him at length about my goals and desires. Through this conversation we discovered that we were very much on the same page. What he brought to the table was funding for album projects, and also distribution physically and digitally in Japan. Additionally, he partnered with me on a really important band that I formed and co-led with my musical brother, Takeshi Ohbayashi.

Spice of Life and I first worked together on my third album, *Onward and Upward,* and they funded the distribution of my album in Japan. However, the project we really wanted to create, and believed would be impactful for Japanese audiences, was a band called the New Century Jazz Quintet. This band was made up of a hybrid group of American and Japanese players, who were young and emerging from NYC and Japan.

I did this because I recognized that there was a huge gap in the jazz market as far as young American jazz musicians. We subsequently created a project that allowed us to fill that gap. We developed a fixed budget, under 20K for each record, with Sassa securing minimal PR only in Japan. Additionally, he gave us tour support as well, with connections to major clubs and festivals in Japan, and built that into his ability to get his return on investment. While most labels just give you CDs to sell, Sassa went on tour with us, and was able to grow his own network and company. This successful combination and result made this a 360 deal.

As a result of the deal we had with Sassa San, I had achieved the goal of getting my name out in a new market. I recorded four albums as a co-leader with New Century Jazz Quintet, had about five successful tours in Japan, and eventually we launched the first ever jazz camp for young Japanese students interested in studying with American jazz musicians. The camp, Seiko Jazz Camp, which was sponsored by Seiko Watch Company, is still successful to this day under the direction of my friend Mike Dease, along with Tomoki Sassa.

In conclusion, because of my 360 deal with this label, I was able to achieve my goal: good records were funded, distributed, and publicized. Of course, in this case, everything remained in Japan. But this was also part of my plan: as my career began to shift, I wanted to get more visibility in other markets globally and ultimately in the USA, and that's what this deal afforded me. With this kind of record deal, I didn't make any long-term financial gain, but this definitely positively impacted my career profile as a producer, musician, and leader in the Japanese market. All of these elements led to my ultimate success in the US market as well.

Third recording deal

For some of you, it may be difficult to garner a traditional record deal, especially with labels not being able to make their money back on sales completely from their initial investment. Another feasible route could really be the artist paying for the production of their album, and then licensing it to a label nationally or internationally. One of the first jazz musicians who created and worked according to this concept is the great Erroll Garner, along with his manager, Martha Glaser. But there's a third option: there can be a partnership between labels that can bring a particular project to fruition.

Songs of Freedom, a star-studded full-fledged project that I was working on, needed funding from a much larger budget than most boutique labels offer or I could afford. But I was able to work out partnership to bring the project into reality. This record turned out to be a partnership with DiskUnion Japan and Resilience Music Alliance, a US record label.

First some relative background: most boutique labels are going to want you to keep your album budgets under $10K, and make it very much all in with mixing/mastering and very limited PR campaigns. So, if you want to make heftier-budget albums—as in my case—with budgets over $15K, and even beyond $20K, you are going to need the support of larger labels. Additionally, keep in mind that once the record is completed, you are going to want aggressive PR campaigns with major companies that are going to get to secure print, digital, and radio campaigns for you. Note—and I'll be talking about this soon—one successful PR campaign can change your career for the positive, so PR is almost as hugely important as the other production elements.

I was fortunate to accomplish those goals successfully, and I am incredibly thankful to DiskUnion and Resilience for helping to make my dreams a reality. Also, during this time, I formed a great relationship with Unlimited Myles, my managing and booking agency, and we needed to have the full support for touring. *Songs of Freedom* was my first album with full support and an "engine" to assist me with those goals and visions.

It's really important to not only have a musical vision, but a PR vision for your music, and also regarding booking—understanding what your full desires are, because in the ideal world, the label, booking agent, and management work in tandem to shift your career and profile to the next level.

You pay for music, the label handles everything else

In this new day and age, a lot of labels are looking for artists to have some skin in the game, and many times they will create a licensing deal with your product as long as you have paid for a key component of the recording. There is a jazz record label that I have a great deal of respect for, and they are creating great product, and have built a nice catalogue within the jazz community. Their model is that you, as the artist, pay your musicians for your recording, and they will pay for the studio, mixing, and promotional/marketing costs. They have a great in-house system and it has helped in promoting each artist who is on their roster.

As far as your own recording deals, as mentioned above, there are some recording options—and here are some other ways you can deal with the production of your own work, plus the options and elements you need to consider:

- Fund your own records
- Own your masters
- Seek a powerful digital distribution company
- See if the label or you yourself can fund a powerful PR company and strategy.
- Secure a booking agent so you can work and sell your own records on the road, and at the very least you can make money as a touring audience and build your fan base.
- And this brings me to my next point:

Starting your own label

If you go this route, you have to really have a cohesive business model—one that involves patience and time for the label to grow, and a musical aesthetic that will allow you over time to make an impact in the industry. Within my field of jazz, there are many of my colleagues who have successfully started a label, and continue to maintain it with success:

- Dave Douglas—Greenleaf Records
- Willie Jones III—WJ3 Records
- Branford Marsalis—Marsalis Music
- John Bishop—Origin Records
- Marc Free and Nick O'Toole—Posi-Tone Records
- Nick Finzer—Outside in Music

- José James—Rainbow Blonde Records

Even some larger institutions have done something similar, where they have utilized the reach and power of the organization to distribute and fund their own live music catalogue.

- Blue Train Records—Jazz at Lincoln Center
- SF Jazz Records—SF Jazz Collective

In my personal experience, I been asked many times if I wanted to start my own label. Actually, for a few years in my early production career, I had my own record company called Sound on Purpose Records. We functioned as a moniker and a label imprint that gave artists a way to not completely look like they were self-releasing their product. However, this route requires a lot a lot of capital to sustain the costs of running a record label. The friends and colleagues I know who have done this successfully have had another funding source or job that they could rely upon while waiting for the success of the label to multiply into something substantial.

OPTIONS AND CONSIDERATIONS IN PRODUCTION AND PRE-PRODUCTION

Now that I have explained many different models, let's consider what you need from a label and really understand what the various labels offer.

The label handles:

- Recording costs (musicians, studios, engineers)
- PR (various plans)
- Digital and physical distribution
- Artist-purchased additional product (there is a buy back policy with most labels that will also be part of your contract so the label can get back some of their investment in your album costs)

WHAT IS A PRODUCER?

"The producer knows who to call, and who should be in the room."—Quincy Jones

This—knowing who to call and who should be in the room—is a key attribute for a producer. The first time I recall directly hearing the term producer was from Greg Knowles, who has been a great resource to me and one of the first people ever to say I had potential as a producer in the business. One of the first things that made him affirm me as a producer was that I was resourceful, and he felt that I had ears that were beyond just being able to hear myself; he said I could hear others and what could make the music better.

Know that a producer just isn't a person who tells people what to do. They are people who get the right team and musicians in the room. There is also a great deal of planning and understanding of music and concepts that it takes to be a producer. After all, they need to get the balance of it all: music, the studio, musicians, personalities, project planning, and the understanding of the musical market and what's out there. This will help the producer effectively steer the artist in the right direction based on their vision for their careers.

Producers are very powerful, and can make a total difference in your career. If you have the right producer, he or she can help you unveil aspects of your own artistry.

How can you find the right producer? Take the time to get educated about the person you're considering hiring. Make sure that person gets all that this type of project entails, ideally with a stellar track record. After all, this is a person that you will have to trust and who will make the process of making an album so much easier because of their own knowledge and experience.

As I've mentioned before, I find that some of the best producers are musicians who understand the business side of making records. Some of my favorite producers are Robert Sadin, Quincy Jones, Larry Klein, Charles Stepany, and Tommy LiPuma—and there are more!

WHAT IS A PRODUCTION COMPANY?

Essentially, a production company is one that pulls together a great team of people working towards the same goal. Again—it's about relationship building, in this case, with people who you not only get along with, but those who have the talent that you need.

One of my favorite filmmakers is the Oscar-winning Spike Lee. If you are as big a Spike fan as I, you most likely realize that so many of his movies, no matter the genre, have had the same actors and behind-the-camera crew during the last twenty-five years of his film-making career. He has a consistent team of people whom he loves to work with and who bring his vision to life. That's exactly how I work with my production team.

I decided to start my production company because I realized that producing a record took more than just myself to be part of the project. I needed to have a team of engineers, graphic artists, photographers, videographers, and musicians whom I could consistently call on to assemble projects. I've been lucky enough to make that happen; we have a great synergy and we trust each other. In our case, it's also not our first rodeo, so we understand how to work together. It's great to have a team I can trust and count on, one that will work towards the musical results needed to complete whatever project we choose to make the focus of our efforts.

Even when I'm working with new clients, for whom it may take a bit to get how we work, they can quickly see that we have a chemistry—and history.

WHAT IS A CO-PRODUCTION?

Essentially, a co-production is a joint venture between at least two production companies. This type of arrangement can give the artist the best of both worlds by having producers who excel in different areas and together contribute to stellar expertise. It can result in a dynamic and powerfully successful experience for all.

Over the last few years, when I've had a chance to produce for major labels and work with artists who have a broader reach and following than I did earlier in my career, I decided to work with a few co-producers on certain albums. The last few records I have co-produced have been with producers who have way more experience at making records than myself, and they have educated me on many things. What I brought to the table was my ability to really assemble a team, setup the sessions, bring solidified album concepts, and also enforce the production agenda from inside the booth as a player. Again, we exhibited different yet compatible strengths: my co-producing partner sat behind the mixing board with the engineer, being able to hear the big picture of what's going on, and I got to be "inside the ring," making musical decisions that helped bring the vision to life.

My advice with co-production teams is to make some clear decisions prior to starting the project. Decide who will play what role, and handle certain things, and allow each producer to own their part of the process. In doing so, everything gets done and is covered. Additionally, it's important to work out financial agreements and royalties with the co-producer based on the percentage everyone agrees upon.

WHAT ARE THE STEPS FOR MAKING A RECORDING OR EP?

Before I answer that, let's define some relevant terms.

- **Album:** An album is a collection of material, usually totalling between fifty and sixty minutes in length, that can fit on a CD. Before, when they were placed on LPs, they were shorter in length. Typically, an album includes several tracks, though this is contingent upon the genre.
- **EP:** EP, which is short for extended play, refers to a recoding that has more tracks than just a single, but is still too short to be an album.
- **Single:** A single is one track of recorded music, and is typically under five minutes.

Now that we have those defined, let's get into the steps.

Many artists have still not chosen to make their first album, single, or EP because they are fearful about the necessary steps to take. Below is a laundry list of questions that will lead to necessary steps to make sure your record is completed and with excellence. You can choose to shortcut this process, but it will show itself later down the road if you choose to.

Why are you making this record?

It's important to unpack your *why* behind making a record. It's similar to choosing to have and care for a baby: everyone might want to hold a beautiful new baby when the parents walk into the room, but not many people really want to endure what they went through from conception to delivery. In the sense of wanting to attain something without getting the clear reasoning of why, you can compare that to making an album. If an artist can't give me a legitimate reason why they should make a record, then I tell them to wait until they have a defined objective, or, in my experience, they won't have the endurance to see the dream through. I can tell you countless stories about artists who started the process and didn't complete it primarily because they weren't connected to the *why* that would aid them in finishing the project.

What do you want to say musically?

One of the greatest pleasures I have is when I encounter an artist who absolutely knows what he or she wants to say but needs help saying it. In those cases, it's just a matter of getting the right arrangers, composers, and band around to help bring that vision to life. However, if you want to make a record, and you don't really know what you want to say musically, again, my question would be, "Why do you need to make a record, and why now?"

How many songs do you want to record?

Pre-production is one of the most integral parts of planning a record, and many artists who want to skip past pre-production and go straight into the recording studio worry me greatly. After all, this is when the real planning and thought process is analyzed to the greatest degree. One of my mentors told me that when he used to work on the production team for Nancy Wilson and the record company she was part of, they started the meetings with over 100 songs to consider. From that list of 100 songs, they narrowed them down to the twelve to fifteen tracks that made it to the record.

Though I love gathering from a large repertoire of songs to choose from, the alternative is also great. For example, when you have an artist who has ten to twelve songs or less that they feel are musts for an album, that's also exciting. Either way, it's important to consider what material you want on the album, and also to try to make sure each of the songs has a relationship to the others and that, ultimately, they work together to achieve the overarching goal of the album concept.

Who is going to be part of this record?

Another part of pre-production is considering who is going to be on the album. This is key, because many of the great records that we have loved and adored from the beginning of recording history have had everything to do with who was in the room and collaborating on the project.

Choose musicians who also can help you reach your goals in the studio. There is a difference between musicians who play live well, and musicians who understand how to translate their musicality for the studio. These are two different approaches to playing vs. recording, which is why you have the term "session" musicians to describe musicians who are great in that realm. Again, you want to choose carefully according to your project.

How much are you paying the band?

It's crucial to consider what you are going to pay the band in pre-production. This goes back to a conversation we had earlier when I mentioned planning ahead. I strongly disagree with people who plan an entire recording process and strategy and then, at the last minute, consider what the band needs. After all, it's the band that's going to be in the heat of the battle with you and working hard in real time to make this record special.

It's important to decide on what the fee will be from the beginning. This includes, in my opinion, paying the band the day of the session. And speaking of payment, sometimes, with larger labels, they may delay the payment due to accounting reasons. However, if I am producing, I want every musician going home that day, after having played their hearts out, with a check. Sidebar: it's also great to feed the band because, again, they are working hard and their spirit and energy is what will make this album something unique. Consider them as they consider you.

Are you hiring a producer?

I spoke about this earlier, but depending on the stage and vision you may already have, you may opt out of having a producer, but it's something that should be part of your discussion and pre-production conversation.

How much are you paying the producer?

Every producer has a different way that they like to be paid. In general, they may charge a day rate, or for the entire project, though there are slight variances to both methods. Early in my production career, and depending on the scale of the project, I preferred to charge a flat fee. Some producers for larger-scale projects charge a fee that includes points on the record towards royalties as well. Again, it just depends on the workload and the level of producer you are working with, and what you're both or all comfortable with.

Where are you making this record?

Many recording studios are closing by the day due to the fact that you can go to Guitar Center, Sam Ash, or even Sweetwater and order as much gear as you need. The other day I was recording vocal overdubs for an artist, and we powered up a laptop with Pro Tools, had an interface and a high-quality microphone ready, and began recording at my apartment. The difference, though, is the sound and engineering of the room, and most of the studios that are still open have ideal acoustics, and, most importantly, a history of recording great records. Which is why people are still making records at Sear Sound, Bunker

Studios, Big Orange Sheep, Trading 8s Music, Capital Studios, and Electric Lady Studios, and the many studios that are still around. However, it's important to analyze the budget and factor in the studio cost. Some musicians may opt to record in a well-equipped home studio in a smaller city so that they have more time and can record without counting their pennies.

There is no ideal scenario that works for all; it boils down to preference for the artist and to the sonic goal they have in mind. When I produce an artist, I ask them to bring several records that they consider great albums for us to listen to together. It's important to identify the albums that give you the feeling that you love. Once you have done that, then research where those artists recorded, and then speak to their engineers, to understand their recording process. All of that matters when considering the results you want to achieve.

How much does the studio cost?

Studio rates vary, especially depending on the location, which I spoke about earlier. It's important to speak to the studio ahead of time and get their rates, so you can factor that in while in the planning and pre-production stages.

Who is going to mix and master your records?

This is a huge key to making records. "Fix it in the mix," is B.S. You cannot fix what you do not properly take the time to prepare in the beginning of the process. Finding the right mixing and mastering engineer is key, and just like it's important to research what studios you love based on the albums that you really like, it's equally important to do the research on who has mixed and mastered those records as well. Note that there are a lot of the same names on great records.

Are you going to print CDs or LPs?

These days, because of the decline in CD sales, I don't advise anyone to purchase a large amount of CDs. I can show you various closets and storage places in my home that have CDs that have not been sold, but again, that's me. My friend Alicia Olatuja can't keep enough CDs in her home because she is on tour way more than me and her fan base still loves buying her CDs and having her sign them. I would really look at the amount of touring you have coming up in your career, and measure that with how many CDs you should order.

LPs are a very specialized product and market, and, as I stated earlier, thanks to consumer patterns, they are on the rise again. In fact, because of this rebirth in LP sales, you can charge more to your audience for them because they cost more (pressing LPs is quite costly— and a therefore a huge investment for a smaller amount of product). The average price you can charge at a concert for a CD is $20-$25, while for LPs at a concert, you can charge up to $40.

Who are you hiring for PR?
I'll be addressing PR in Chapter 8, but this is important to consider here. There is a lot of competition: get multiple offers from PR firms, and figure out if they really want to represent who you are and your project, versus just wanting another client on their roster. Consider their knowledge about where you are in your career, and how their wisdom and experience can positively impact your project and career.

Who are you hiring for radio?
Some say that radio is a lost art, but I disagree; it's just changed mediums. Radio is still very important for touring and for getting a name in various territories around the country especially. Choosing the right radio person, one who has access to the right stations, is key.

Where are you going to coordinate a CD release event or tour?
If you are a new artist, I want to save you time and frustration by offering this advice: stop looking for a booking agent. I say this because I wasted years trying to secure one and wasn't ready for one. It wasn't until I had a big project at a major venue that an agent could actually sell that one pursued me.

Before a point like that in your career, it's going to be difficult and close to impossible to just get a booking agent, since they only make money when you make money. Unless you have big buzz or PR already surrounding your career, it's better to just go ahead and create relationships with various venues and start booking gigs and setting up your own CD release event and tour. Trust me: when it's time, a booking agent will seek you out. At that point, you need to make sure they are reputable, honest, and realistic about what they can do for you. If they are asking you for money on day one, then I would question their motives.

How long can you work this record?

The release time of your record is key, because it allows you to work the record for a period of time. If you release an album in October, it's going to be very difficult to keep the momentum of that record going during the holidays. However, if you release your album in February, you have multiple quarters and months to re-imagine your album.

Also, it's important to know that many venues book months and, in some cases, years in advance. You'll want to consider timing so that you can best capitalize on the market. For example, let's say you do release an album in February—you might not get a steady stream of gigs until the fall, which is actually a good period of time.

What is the power of publishing?

Publishing is not an area I am an expert in, but one worth exploring. My friend worked at ASCAP for many years, and he spoke about the power of publishing and its ability to economically sustain musicians. This, dear students, is something you may want to consider right away. For younger musicians who are in college, begin a relationship with publishing companies even now, because they have competitions and awards that can be helpful to you at this stage of your career.

Vincent Herring, a legendary jazz alto saxophonist, always said to me, "Ulysses, make sure you take the time to compose your own music, because that is literally like purchasing real estate." It's the gift that keeps on giving, especially when you are fortunate to get your music submitted for major projects that have financial gain.

Frankly, it's the one part of my career that I really need to put more energy into. What I will say is that years ago, I would hear stories about musicians like Herbie Hancock, Marcus Miller, and many great composers like Lalo Schifrin and beyond who, due to their income thanks to publishing, don't have to work another day in their careers.

If there is more information you seek about publishing your material, you should research ASCAP, BMI, and SESAC, which are legitimate and long-standing publishing companies that support many of the world's great songwriters in multiple genres. There are some artists that even start their own publishing companies as well, and have been very successful. Again, I am not an expert in this area, but merely want to have this be part of the book so that you can be aware of it and do your own research.

Copyright

Copywriting your material is so important these days, especially given the reality of streaming, YouTube, and so many digital outlets and how they are freely distributing material via the Internet. It's so easy to just compose music or create material and not seek to go through the same labor to protect yourself. However, there are many musicians whose lives have changed for the worse because they didn't protect their work. Again, this is where an entertainment lawyer would be very helpful.

In conclusion, I've given you a lot of food for thought regarding deals and recording in this chapter. Take your time with it; read and review as needed. And be patient: there's a lot to learn, but when you're motivated—as I think you are—it's an interesting and key part of this path that you're choosing.

Reflections for thought and discussion:

1. How can you get your music out there?
2. What method would be best for you to record your work?

3. What would you tell someone if they asked you why you wanted to record an album?
4. Could you possibly raise the money you need to fund your album?
5. What albums do you admire most and who's worked on them?
6. How can you develop a relationship with a producer and/or publisher?

Reflections for writing:

1. Write the name of three producers whom you admire, along with the work they've done.
2. What are the different skills that they have that you would like to possess?
3. Consider your goal in recording. Based on the steps/considerations outlined in this chapter, create a timeline with the steps you'll need to take in order to get there. Use the following to help guide you:
   - Title of project
   - Artist
   - Goal of album or project
   - Timeline
   - Pre-production
   - Rehearsals
   - Recording
   - Post-production
   - Date to send product to PR
   - Release date

CHAPTER 7
Endorsements

When I was about sixteen years old, my hardworking parents had
saved some money for me to buy a new drum kit. The Yamaha Maple
Custom Absolute kit had just come out and I was dying to try it. At
the time, there was a great music store in Orlando, Florida, called
Thoroughbred Music Store, and they were really cool about letting
people try out the instruments and pairing people with the right
instrument based on skill-set and potential. They suggested that
my parents purchase this Yamaha Kit. I fell in so in love with those
drums that I wanted more than to play the instrument; I wanted
to pursue a formal relationship with the company. That was when I
first got interested in the concept of endorsements. Since then, I've
learned a lot—and this is what I want to share with you here.

Because the level of expectations didn't match the level of career
I had attained that point, this incident sparked a lot of heartache,
confusion, and, fortunately, subsequent learning. Bottom line: It's
important to have realistic expectations for a company, and to be
honest about the level of value you have to offer them. Also, there has
to be room for you on the roster. For example, in my case, because
Yamaha is such a large, highly popular, and respected company, there
were so many drummers already fulfilling a similar vision on their
roster.

At this point, I am fortunate to have over ten endorsement and
sponsorship relationships across multiple types of companies. I'm
lucky to have partnerships with companies that believe and invest

fully in me. Additionally, I truly enjoy the sound of their products; the relationship is mutually beneficial, which is what an endorsement should be.

Let me go back and define what endorsements mean, as well as give you some key relevant tips.

WHAT ARE ENDORSEMENTS?

Endorsements are when a company values your talent in a way that they want to form a direct relationship with you that will allow you to promote their product as part of your brand. Part of that relationship may include free product, their support in your touring and educational efforts, and, in some cases, even the opportunity to collaborate in the creation of some new products with them.

Companies, especially now, have bottom-line figures that they need to reach, and they are targeting artists who can assist with that. Also, due to the increase of social media and consumers being influenced by social media, brands are watching the social media profiles of musicians and using that as part of the consideration of who they will sponsor and endorse.

It is definitely a major stamp of affirmation when a company seeks you out to work with them. However, make sure you bring something to the table as well.

RULES OF ENGAGEMENT WITH ENDORSEMENTS
First and foremost, find the instrument that you actually love to play.

Do not make yourself settle and play an instrument because there is some potential you may get it for free. Belief should go beyond convenience. I've developed my own test: if I am willing to pay for the product and have paid for the product, then I know that I want to endorse the product.

Look realistically at the company and be self-critical and ask, do I fit the roster?

Make sure there is room for you and your musical aesthetic. For instance, at Yamaha, they already had so many great younger jazz drummers who were very similar to what I brought to the table, so I understood why they weren't fully interested. Also, at that time, everyone wanted to be signed by Yamaha, and quite frankly, they could afford to be picky, because people were going to buy the product regardless because of the company's reputation in the industry.

Don't be needy—or try to beg your way onto the roster.

I have always told artists, "Don't become so dependent on trying to gain the attention from certain companies; they can smell the blood, like a shark. When they sense that attitude, it repels them, and they don't want anything to do with you." Most companies these days will approach me and ask me to become interested in their product, because, ultimately, I don't need any of the relationships to make music. Companies are not that affected by your personality, though artists do play an important role in product visibility. In general, it's helpful to approach companies with a collaborative spirit and a high level of humility. Focus on your talent and your work ethic.

Put yourself in the company's shoes.

Imagine you owned a company and you had a limited inventory, and you needed to qualify and quantify every time you decided to give product away to someone. You would be very careful, just like how you decide when you're going give money away or make a donation. You make sure you believe in the person, or the organization. You measure their progress, and/or determine if they will actually progress from your generosity. I find that when I behaved with this thought in mind, when I showed that I understood their side of the equation, company reps actually loved having me around.

Remove your ego from the conversation.

I was having dinner one night with reps from a well-known companies, and they were telling me about their trials and tribulations after attending the National Association of Music Merchants (NAMM). This is a trade show for music manufacturers and distributors to get a sneak peek at new gear that the companies are releasing. NAMM also gives distributors a chance to make early sales and decide what they will stock in the coming months. Endorsing artists are also invited to this event, which makes it otherwise known as a cattle call for young musicians who want to get signed by companies. So, for those of us who are already signed, it's a chance to catch up with the reps who care for us during the year. However, for musicians who aren't signed, this is a chance for them to get to know potential endorsers.

The reps—at that dinner—started recounting their tales. They told me stories of artists walking up to them, touting their tour schedules and who they're recording with. They were complaining that the musicians who were, in a way, "begging" for attention often spoke with a sense of entitlement—expecting that by sharing their tour schedules, companies would immediately send crates of gear to their homes.

In conclusion, as far as endorsements, here's my best advice: be kind, play on a high level, seek to have visible musical scenarios, always be improving and getting better, and the right companies will find you.

Reflections for thought and discussion:

1. What endorsement relationships would you like to have?
2. What companies are you considering?
3. Do you just want the gear, or do you believe in the mission? Explain.
4. Do you fit the roster?
5. What about your social media presence demonstrates that you are ready to represent one of your chosen companies?
6. What do you need to do to get your social media presence primed for that position?

Reflections for writing:

1. Write down three companies you are interested in possibly representing.

2. How can you approach them? Write down at least three ways of reaching them.

3. For each company, write a short and targeted email that you could send to them to sell yourself as an excellent endorsement candidate.

CHAPTER 8

Public Relations

Public relations is all about getting you out to your audience. There are many branches to this very important part of the success of your professional music career, and every seasoned artist has his or her own tale to tell. Here I'm sharing my experience, my relevant tips and advice for you so that you are prepared for this crucial component of your success.

And there's not one answer for everyone. For example, one of my dear friends is a very talented and well-known artist who has, for the past several years, had a PR agent on consistent retainer while she performs and tours. This kind of long-term PR representation gives her the opportunity to maximize and capitalize on her success. Depending on your career, and the level of opportunities that you are greeted with, there may be a season where you may desire to have a PR team on retainer to promote various opportunities you may have.

Public relations can be a confusing area for the new—or even seasoned—musician. A good PR person can generate big buzz for their artists. But how do you find this perfect PR person? Here I'm sharing some tips to guide you as you delve into your search for a PR person who matches your personality—and budget.

First, my PR backstory: Kari Gaffney, a wonderful woman who is still representing artists, was my first PR representative. Kari called me one day when I had just released my first album, *It's Time for U*, and we spoke about the need for PR. I really didn't understand the purpose and reasoning behind PR, especially because I just didn't have the money to afford the service.

I said to her, "Kari, I don't really have any more money to invest in this album; I just want to get the music heard."

She then replied, "Ulysses, your music will be heard, but not by that many people, and you will have invested all of that money, and no one will know about your record."

So, I reasoned with myself, and thought, "What's a few extra dollars to make sure that I am able to have people hear the record, and have writers and publications write about the record?" Dear students, that was the right decision. Kari took the time to educate me on the world of PR as an independent artist, and how to effectively start that journey. Thanks to her campaign, I was able to gain an audience I would never have reached otherwise.

Over the years, I have found value in various PR representatives and companies, and understand that much of where I currently am in my career has a great deal to do with the level of traction they were able to facilitate.

PR AGENT

I've just described my very positive experience with Kari. Well, the same goes for you: it's important to find the right PR agent—someone who has the time and energy to devote to you and your project. How can you find the right PR agent? Referrals are good. Also, make sure you're prepared with a strategy (more on that in the next section) and have some ideas of what you'd like to do. Trust your gut; a lot of times, finding the person who "gets" you is all about the chemistry you have when you meet.

One other thing to understand, however, is that you won't be their only client. They will probably have your project and others that they are working on simultaneously because they have to make a living, just like you, and it's very difficult for them to do so just by working with one client at a time. Don't be offended by the reality that you aren't alone on their roster. Just make sure they have a clear and individual strategy for your project, as well as room to work on your project as much as possible.

STRATEGY DOCUMENT

As I mentioned, you will need to build your own strategy document prior to meeting your potential PR rep and/or company. Get your laptop out, or even a sheet of paper and a pen, and do the following:

Write the various publications you want to target.

If you're not sure, look at artists who have a similar sound to what you're creating, and emulate some of their strategic moves. Keep in mind, of course, that everyone's music is different, and the way that the industry will respond to you will be different than how they respond to others.

Think outside the box.

Dream big and think of new publications and blogs to target. For instance, in the jazz world, there are certain publications that every musician vies to get attention from. As challenging as it might be to get into these publications, there's no harm in reaching for the sky. Think of an interesting angle that could get a writer interested in pulling you in—and perhaps reach a new audience the publication is trying to find.

Review and consider your goals.

Ask yourself what the results that you would feel completely satisfied with would be. Before you sign your PR contract, send them this list. Examine both their reaction and whether or not they have a track record for the kind of goals you have. If they don't, the relationship could be problematic. Conversely, it's important that you be both realistic and flexible about your expectations.

Share your expectations for feedback from the start.

Think about how often you'd like to get updates from your PR people. Weekly? Bi-weekly? Don't let them hide behind a, "Well, we pitched what we could" statement and then run off with your hard-earned money. Hold their feet to the fire, but be honest with realistic expectations on what they can actually accomplish for you—and when.

Though I'm not going to share the company names here, I did want to share some of my relevant PR experience so that you can see some of the possibilities in that realm.

PR COMPANY POSSIBILITIES—AND EXPECTATIONS: MY STORY

Again, there are so many different ways to approach PR. I want to share three of my campaigns with you here.

PR Campaign #1

I was new to making records, and this PR representative literally "got in the sand" with me and took my music and project personally, like it was their own. When they began to pitch the project, it was as though they produced the record themselves; they really were committed to me and the process. The results weren't large, but they were steady. I could measure and track their success, and I felt their support completely through the whole campaign. As a result, I constantly refer new artists, who are beginning their first PR campaign, and who completely need to be supported, to this company.

PR Campaign #2

This campaign was the most expensive one for me. In retrospect, at the time, I should have had one of those mirror talks with myself to figure out if my ego was distorting my perspective. Of course, when I look back, I can see what happened: when I released this particular project, I had very specific goals that were honestly very ego-driven. Because I felt like I wasn't releasing my first record anymore, and I had been on some high-profile projects, and been featured in certain publications already, I felt that I was at a particular level. In my mind, I thought I just needed a record and the right PR agent, and everything else was going to be great.

But that's not the way it happened.

Again, looking back, there were signs. For example, the first red flag was that they signed several artists who had similar projects, and our projects were basically competing with each other's in the mainstream market. From a PR perspective, they felt it was great, because they had several great artists. However, from my perspective, it meant the publications had to choose between the artists, and they constantly did not choose me.

In spite of this, I garnered a few write-ups that have been critical to my bio/résumé, and I am thankful for that, but it was not worth the price tag. Consequently, that PR agent and I honestly didn't have the best relationship for a while. I don't think they were bad people, but our relationship didn't feel as if it had an honest foundation; I felt taken advantage of. Again, looking back, I realize that I arrived at their doorstep desperate and eager, which is a dangerous combination! I didn't trust my gut instinct.

However, I am thankful for the experience, because it gave me just that: experience. Additionally, I hope that this will help those of you who are reading this, who don't have to make the same mistakes I made. One of the lessons learned: trust your gut, and take your time. Don't rush into an agreement. If too much is promised, or it seems too good to be true, it probably is.

PR Campaign #3

This campaign was probably the best experience I had with a PR agent beyond my first campaign. From day one, this PR agent was on. It started with a request: "Ulysses, send me what your expectations are, and let me look them over." They promptly replied with a list of things that I needed to change in my PR materials and approach to social media first. Additionally, they told me that they could realistically accomplish between 40% and 50% of my expectations because, as they put it, "Your career is still growing, and so are we!" However, they did create a model of PR that was realistic, and delivered based on the expectations they set. I still recommend them to new artists because of their clarity and integrity.

This experience also taught me a lot. What I learned is that you can hire a top-tier PR company, but if your materials, image, and brand are not together, there is a limit as far as what they can do for you.

OTHER WAYS TO GAIN PR

As is the case in many realms, there are several DIY options for PR. Recently, I had a talk a friend from a PR agency and they explained to me how so much in the publicity world is shifting, largely due to social media. This person gave me great advice: we as artists need to create new partnerships outside of our normal relationships and thereby leverage the brand reach and power with our brand. If you look at the sports industry, pop and mainstream world, they have been doing that for years. They obviously have their news outlets, but ultimately, as I mentioned in Chapter 7, one endorsement relationship can open up a whole new following for an artist.

In my case, I had the luck of connecting with a clothing company. A couple of years ago, I was approached by a clothing company that really loved my image and brand on social media and wanted to partner with me. From that partnership, I was able to get some great video and social content, and a professional photo shoot that not only boosted my media profile, but also allowed other brands to approach me. The level of promotion and exposure to a new audience that I received from those campaigns were completely beyond any level of PR campaign that I had ever had access to on my own, especially within the jazz world.

But let's get back to you—and what can work for you.

CONSIDERATIONS FOR THE DEVELOPMENT OF YOUR PR MATERIALS

The key players in PR are people I've mentioned previously: publicists and PR agencies.

But what many will see—and what you need to take the lead on in many cases, especially in the beginning—are your PR materials. Here are a few points for you to keep in mind as you develop these materials:

Grammar matters

Grammar is important; your writing represents you. My advice? Please pay someone to edit your bio. If you don't have access to an editor, find an English teacher or someone who can help you for free. My bio has gone under various revisions through the years, and I have had many different people give me great advice about how to organize my information with my bio. A huge part of it is knowing how to frame things grammatically, as well as word choices, on top of how to properly list your credentials.

But even before you hand it over to someone else to review, read it aloud. You'll be surprised at how much this helps. When you read aloud, you can catch some of your own errors, and repetitions. If you are using the same words over and over, take a look at a thesaurus to help you. You want to be fresh—and not redundant.

Bio, résumé, and CV

As I've mentioned in Chapter 3, a bio is necessary as a creative for multiple platforms: applications for jobs, colleges, and grants, as well as a variety of opportunities. It's important within the short bio format not to lose the power in your professional journey, and to work hard to keep the "meat" of your career still very much on the page. I think it's also helpful to constantly update and re-tool your bio, and look at other templates as well for new ways to keep the bio fresh.

Résumés and CVs, as mentioned earlier, are also important to keep up to date with your work experience, accomplishments, productions, and more. This will help the reader understand the breadth and scope of your career and work.

Electronic press kits

This was something that used to confuse me when I first started collecting materials as a bandleader for booking opportunities. An E.P.K. (not to be confused with promo videos for an album) is for booking agents, managers, and promoters to come to your site and have a set of material that is primarily for them, and includes all of the necessary documents, reviews, and information to procure performance opportunities.

Website

I have had a website since I was about sixteen years old, thanks to a family friend, Al Reshard. Even back then, he told me that it was important for me to have an online web presence that displayed my information to those whom I'd never had contact with. I was lucky to have Al because websites, back then, were way more complicated and quite pricey.

Today, it's much easier and more economical to do it yourself. If you have a concept and domain name, companies like Wix, SquareSpace, and many others can facilitate the process of getting you a site. And most of them allow you to pay a monthly subscription. Still, if you have a contact who knows about navigating the whole website thing, go to him or her for guidance. After all, a website represents you, so you want it to shine. And, dear students, please note that social media—though crucial in our life—is not a website. Don't think you're saving money by not having a website; it's definitely an important investment. While promoters and potential clients will definitely look at your social media page to see what activities you are up to professionally, a website is the place that holds a lot of information about who you are in greater and more formal detail.

Depending on your field or area of focus, your website will evolve in a particular way as far as what it presents to your audience. You should feel free to, as I do, reference other people's sites and borrow ideas from them. You might even need additional tabs if you have various other parts of your career that require their own pages.

Headshot

I want to go back to something I spoke about Chapter 3: your headshot.

This is another category where I feel artists really try to cut corners, and as a result, they don't have the best images of themselves on the web. I remember a photographer who was a friend of mine pulled me aside one day and really gave some tough criticism about my photos. She said to me, Google yourself, and look at the inconsistency of the quality of your images.

She said to me, "Ulysses, based on the goals that you say you have as an artist, and to one day be a bandleader—you can't afford to *not* look presentable consistently."

So, I not only worked on my image off-stage, but then I got with photographers as well for headshots and really made sure my photos matched the brand goals and visions I have for myself. Also, hire a photographer who knows how to help you pose and achieve good lighting, and who has access to a good studio, or really good locations for outside shots.

Finally, image quality is also huge: as an artist, I would implore you to not make a headshot from your iPhone. It's really helpful to get a high-res photo from a DSLR camera. In doing so, the photos transferred to websites, programs, and additional outlets where your media will be utilized will be sharp. You will probably also want to have someone use Adobe Photoshop to perfect the picture. Again, great pictures matter, trust me, and having them will allow you to be considered for things that you may not ordinarily be considered for.

The band

If you are in a group or a band, then it's really important that you get those shots, too. Coordinate the concept and make sure everyone in the band visually looks right so it doesn't look like only half the group knew the stylistic choices. Work with a photographer who can bring out the best in the group. Also, it's really important to have fun!

You can do a lot yourself in this area, too. For example, when I first formed New Century Jazz Quintet with Takeshi, we hired a young photography student, and that worked out well because we were so particular about what we wanted in terms of images, that honestly, she just needed to point and shoot. I styled the band, we found a rooftop on a building, and we came up with some really cool photographic moments that I still love to this day that captured the energy and spirit of the band.

In conclusion—I want to summarize what must be on your website:

1. Bio/About page
2. Shows/Tour Dates page
3. Music page
4. Video page
5. Contact page
6. Photos (both headshots and group photos)

In closing this chapter about PR, as I stated earlier, you want to make sure that you are able to receive quantifiable results from the potential PR campaigns that you invest your dollars into, and the only way to do that is to truly have a vision and goals for your campaign.

Dear students, don't simply walk blindly into an agreement with a company. Write a vision, and a goal list for the campaign, and be honest with the company. Make sure they can fulfill your vision so the relationship becomes a win-win one for all.

Reflections for thought and discussion:

1. Do you personally know someone who has either a positive of negative PR experience. What made it bad or good?
2. What describes a PR person or company you would hire? Explain.
3. Google yourself: Based on your Internet presence so far, is your brand image consistent?
4. Can you improve the quality of your/your group's online images? Explain.
5. Look at the website of a musician that you know/admire/ are similar to. What elements would you like to emulate? Be specific.

6. Do you have a website? Does it have the elements listed in this chapter? How can you—will you—improve it?

Reflections for writing:

1. Look at the strategy document section.
2. Write down at least three publications you'd like to target.
3. Write down at least three publications or blogs that are stars in your musical field. How could you get them interested in you? Write relevant notes/ideas.
4. Write down your PR goals.
5. Write down a list of at least five expectations that you'd have for your PR representation.
6. What are the elements listed in this chapter that you need to either have or improve on? Write a list and a timeline/plan of action, with deadlines. For example, "By June, I'll have my headshots taken."

6. Do you have a website? Does it have the elements listed in this chapter? How can you—will you—improve it?

Reflections for writing

1. Look in the strategy document section
2. Write down at least three publications you'd like to target.
3. Write down at least three magazines or blogs that are sure to your musical field. How could you get them interested in your. Write relevant notes here.
4. Write down your PR goals.
5. Write down a list of at least five expectations that you'd have for your PR representative.
6. What are the five goals listed in this chapter that you'd either buy or improve on? Write the list and go through each of them, with deadlines. For example, here's when I'll have my website fixed.

CHAPTER 9
Touring

We've talked about a lot of ideas relevant to your career as far as what you should prepare for yourself so that the world can "meet you" the way you want people to see you. This brings me to something you've probably thought about: being on the road, or touring. Whether we're talking about a domestic or international tour, it's important to work with a team that can assist you in navigating various challenges. International tours have a different body of expertise needed: local transportation, currency exchange and rates, as well as the overall variables that arrive with being in different time zones and doing business with people in different cultures.

This chapter focuses on navigating the touring world.

WHAT IS A TOUR?

A tour is essentially a chance for you as the artist to bring exposure to your music in multiple destinations, both domestically and internationally. The goal of a tour is also to have a chance to sell your music and build your following via performances at multiple venues like concert halls, clubs, performing arts centers, festivals, and more.

Many argue that touring will be the way you as a professional musician will make money during your career, since, as we've mentioned, the old style of earning isn't what it used to be.

Tours can transition you and your reach beyond what it currently is. It can facilitate the creation of new listening communities. I have seen—and experienced—the power of an effective tour. and its impact on the long-term goals for an artist. I remember that for various artists who I have been fortunate to work with, we would tour with an idea that was just a thought in the artist's mind. And then, by the end of a year of touring, their stature and presence were completely elevated as a result.

Let's now examine your readiness for a tour, as well as the relevant roles.

ARE YOU READY FOR A TOUR?

If you are a young musician, or young within your craft, touring will take your talent to the next level. Most of my personal tour experience has fortunately been with artists who have been on the road for a long time. These musicians possess a high level of artistry that makes audiences around the world want to hear them.

However, most clubs and venues are wary about young talent because their ultimate goal is to sell tickets, and with young talent, they don't have a track record—yet. What does this mean to you? Well, again, you need to be honest with yourself, and assess if you are ready to tour. If you aren't at the level to tour as a leader, the best thing you can do is become a sideman/sidewoman within an ensemble and accompany them as part of a tour, and gain experience by watching others who have the knowledge already.

My first tour experience was on a cruise ship, the summer after my freshman year in college. A representative from Norwegian Cruise lines had come to Juilliard and auditioned musicians to be part of the ship's entertainment, to perform on various tours and fleets. My first run was about seven weeks long, and it was a unique journey. Artistically, it was not the most ideal situation, because I was playing with musicians who had a different pursuit or idea of what it takes to be a great artist, and most of them were seeking merely to make a living. Though they encouraged me, they also teased me for being the young drummer from Juilliard that I was, bright eyed and naïve—wanting to jam all night and listen to records.

That tour taught me a great deal. Playing on a cruise ship was a course in how to play a distinct role in a larger production that was for the purpose of pleasing audiences. It was my first experience on the road of meeting people from different cultures. It was, in addition to being a learning experience, a fruitful and fun one.

The next touring opportunity arose from Juilliard, when they gave me a chance to tour as a student in various countries. That was also a lot of fun. In that case, the school took the helm, and paid the bill, for traveling and making sure we all got to where we needed to go!

WHAT IS A TOUR AS A SIDEMAN?

As a sideman, the goal is to support the lead artist and that artist's vision musically. The responsibility is also to help in creating a consistent show that makes people want to experience your music again and purchase the music. The best sideman knows how to show up on time, make the flights, soundchecks, and call times, on top of playing the music well and not causing drama. As you can imagine, this requires a certain type of personality. If you can do this, you'll be in great company with a select group of people around the world who have been doing this for decades.

WHAT IS A TOUR AS A BANDLEADER?

As a bandleader, touring is quite different because you are juggling so many things. As a leader , your responsibilities include:

- Making sure the band is taken care of;
- Assuring the band manager—if you've got one—is set;
- Creating set lists;
- Reading the audience and delivering a great show; and
- Putting out fires as needed—including any cancellations and subsequent reissuing of tickets, and working with a travel agent.

It's rewarding, but can be stressful, and certainly not for everyone.

I also find that choosing the right band members with great personalities to accompany you and not cause you stress on the road makes things much easier as well.

TOURING AS A LEADER WITH PICKUP BANDS

Sometimes, when the budget is challenging or you are trying to break into a new territory, it's easier to travel by yourself to a new city and work with local musicians. This can allow you to play some of the venues that are ideal for you and connect with the local scene. Additionally, in doing so, a venue has a chance to see what is special about your talent.

Some words of advice here: make sure you are strategic about the music you perform, and also, work with a band that brings out the best in your talent. I didn't follow this advice initially. I was just interested in securing a band, and so I didn't investigate to see if it was working with musicians with whom I had chemistry—or even just some kind of relationship. Remember: every show counts, and this is especially true when you're abroad. My former manager always advised me, "Ulysses, play with people who match your light." I pass these words of wisdom on to you.

As far as finding the right venue, you'll want to find those in which your name will draw an audience. This was something that was very helpful for me to keep in mind when I was in Europe and wanted to further my career as a leader. At that time, I traveled to Italy, France, Greece, and many other destinations to make music with a particular band (through my connections). In doing so, the venue and promoter would become convinced of my talent and consider me for return gigs—with my own band. Again, always, it's about the relationships you build, and, of course, your ability to interact well with people and, obviously, play music!

HOW DO YOU SET UP A TOUR?

The goal of a tour is to focus on an area, or part of a country, or if you are fortunate to have the support of major financial backing, you can hit as many cities as possible. One of your key considerations should be, "Where do I want to go? Who do I want to reach?"

In my case, at this juncture in my career, I have been able to focus on specific regions, and then try to dovetail other venues within that area. So, for instance, if I desire to play the southeast, I'll start with an anchor date: a gig from a performing arts center that pays enough fees for me to pay the band, and their travel. Once I get that, I can call surrounding venues, since I am already in the area, and try to coordinate a concert with them. In doing so, I get to make the most out of my time on the road.

WHO CAN HELP?

If you're new to setting up a tour, you will most likely want—and need—assistance.

The first step in realizing who can help is also considering who has done this before. Even if you aren't at a position in your career to afford assistance from a booking agent, there are great people and even musicians who can act as liaisons in cities and countries where you don't have connections.

Networking for tour assistance

Again and always, my students, it comes back to relationships—and connections. Musicians who have those connections may even allow you to work with them, or share a band that will help you gain access to a new territory. There's no sense in trying to re-invent the wheel. However, there is a lot of sense in using the power of partnership and leverage to accomplish mutually beneficial goals for you and the venues you will develop connections with.

Tour managers

Another option for you could be using a tour manager who manages the tour so that you can perform and focus on the music. They should not function like you or one of your band members. Their job is to focus on all of the logistical necessities so you don't have to. This can be a tedious job, but for those who are gifted enough—as far as organizational skills, details, and interpersonal relations—to do this job, having a tour manager can allow you to have a successful tour.

An adequate tour manager has the experience of having done this job before, and this is really important for you to hear: this is not the time to *try out* a friend or a relative. Of course, some people choose someone they have known for a while to handle this job because of the obvious comfort level that might give you, but that's not the priority you need to keep in mind. A tour manager—especially on your first tours—needs to have professional experience. Otherwise, while you're in the heat of battle, you'll have major issues because of their lack of experience.

What a tour manager needs to be:

A problem solver:
Touring domestically and especially internationally can give rise to lots of potential issues. Your tour manager needs to be able to think quickly on their feet. Especially with traveling, dealing with transportation can be especially challenging. This person needs to quickly grasp local "rules" as far as taking trains, working with local drivers, and, of course, planes, too. You want to feel like the tour manager can handle all of this and essentially tell the band where to go and when to be there.

Flexible and available:
A tour manager needs to constantly be available to you and the band while you're on the road. They don't get an off moment, or a chance to rest. They sleep when everything is handled. And, they also need to know how to keep a certain distance from the band; they don't need to fraternize with them too heavily. It's a special type of balance that a tour manager needs to have.

How do you know if someone is a good tour manager? Well, there are a few key points you need to keep in mind when considering a tour manager:

- Is the person responsible? That means, do they understand the breadth of focus they need to have and the relevant responsibilities as far as all aspects related to being
  on tour? You are going to have to rely on this person as
  far as keeping all the details of the tour first and foremost.
- Can you trust that person with money? A tour manager will collect money for you as far as both your performance fees and your product. You need to be able to trust
  them to not steal from you or the band.
- Is this person committed to the band and you? This is
  the time for a tour manager to show you that you and
  the band come first. A tour manager should not be using
  this moment as the time to get close with everyone else,
  or even the audience. Their number one priority is you
  and your ensemble.
- Is this person emotionally intelligent and sensitive
  enough to be culturally aware and able to handle/
  navigate multiple peoples and personalities? Even in the
  US, there are different business styles, and this is perhaps
  even more true when conducting business abroad. There
  are no definitive rules to learn prior; this is a person who
  has to recognize—respect—and protect your mission, no
  matter where you are!

In conclusion for this chapter, I have two other key touring points
for you to keep in mind as you embark on the touring stage of your
career: transportation and selling product.

TRANSPORTATION

This is probably the largest cost and therefore deterrent as far as a
musician's ability to set up a tour. Transportation costs can certainly
be prohibitive. Being able to front the bill for flights, train tickets, and
rental cars—all expenses that are a major part of what makes a show
possible—is not easy. Despite the fact that most venues will cover

lodging at least for the night of the show, they rarely include travel, so most of the time you'll be dealing with flight buyouts, or a fee that includes an amount that you can contribute to travel.

So, when you are thinking about a tour, you must factor in all of those fees, which will potentially affect your compensation for the gig, especially when you create a standard fee that you want to pay your band. How can you figure this out? Even if you do have the benefit of having assistance from someone, while you're in the tour consideration stage, sit down and plan, and if possible, work towards getting other grants or support that can make it easier for you.

SELLING PRODUCT ON TOUR

Though making money on CDs is very much a lost art, it seems that abroad, people are more inclined to purchase product for two reasons: 1) If they enjoy you and your show, they will want to take something home that chronicles that experience, and 2) They will want to have something that you can sign—so they have memorabilia to share and hopefully continue to pass along to others. Therefore, it's important for you to include a product that has an element of what your audience has experienced that evening, such as a CD that has tunes you played that night.

As Quincy Jones says, "This is the love business. People buy music because you did something in the show that made them fall in love with your craft, and because of that love they feel, they want to always have access to that music and feeling."

Have product that gives your audience that feeling and re-ignites that love until they can experience you again, live!

Reflections for thought and discussion:

1. Have you toured before? What was the experience like?
2. Are you ready for a tour? Explain why you are, or why you aren't, and what you are currently missing.
3. Do you have product for touring? If not, what would you bring?

4. Whom can you currently ask for guidance as far as setting up a tour?

Reflections for writing:

1. What are the top three places you'd like to tour in? Write them down—and also write down why you think those would be great places for you to have a tour.
2. Do you know someone who is a tour manager or could be your tour manager? Write down his or her relevant attributes.
3. Set personal goals related to your own tour. Write down at least five, and how you'll attain them.

PART III

ENTREPRENEURSHIP AND BRANDING

In Part II, I shared a lot of information about the industry you are in, and gave you some ideas of what you'll encounter, from deals to touring. This next section will bring you into two additional crucial areas for you to expand your knowledge base: entrepreneurship and branding, and all the relevant music-industry knowledge you'll need.

Entrepreneurship requires a lot of ingenuity, business savvy, and intuition; branding also requires a skill set that incorporates pragmatism with self-awareness and worldliness. Understanding that overnight sensations rarely happen is one of the underlying principles of this section, which not only reiterates that hard work is needed in order to succeed in this business, but also indicates the step-by-step and practical, results-yielding approach that you can take.

CHAPTER 10

The Laws of Entrepreneurship

Before we dive into this next part, let's talk about what an entrepreneur is.

An entrepreneur is essentially a person who creates and launches a new business idea that begins as a small-scale idea, and eventually turns into something much larger.

I state this definition because, as musicians, we are all quite entrepreneurial by virtue of most of us being classified as freelance artists.

Here, I'm going to share a bit about my early experience in this area. Actually, I've been entrepreneurial since the time I was sixteen years old. Back then, I would pack my drums up in my Chevy Blazer to travel to various gigs, and I'd constantly network within Jacksonville, Florida, looking for work not so much as a sideman, but as a leader. Though I was young, I was lucky enough to know what I wanted. But it's just within the last few years—a couple of decades later—when I've started referring to myself as a creative entrepreneur. Today, I'm happy to report, I find myself in spaces where I have the privilege of constantly creating new options and opportunities for myself and others.

It is my belief that as a musician and creative, if we become more entrepreneurial, we will be able to create more sustainable careers. When an artist isn't thinking in this manner, if someone is not looking for opportunities, and conversely constantly waiting to be hired, and forever putting a career and ability to thrive in the hands of someone else, success—on many levels—will be tougher to attain. Know, dear students, that you deserve better, but you need to reach for it.

If you are reading this book, and you are interested in owning more of your career choices and moves, then this is especially for you. As a result of my personal experience, as well as my interaction with scores of artist and students, I've developed five key questions for thoughtful consideration.

FIVE KEY CONSIDERATIONS FOR THE DEVELOPMENT OF ENTREPRENEURSHIP
What do you want?

As an entrepreneur, you must strive to be clear not only about what you desire, but also how and when you want it. This requires great focus and consideration. By defining your goals and creating a relevant timeline, you can determine the pace and flow of your efforts.

How will you obtain it?

Assess your current relationships and connections to figure out who you already know who can assist you in facilitating the attainment of your goals. Remember, these connections can potentially be people who are not direct contacts, but friends of friends. Make a list, and think about what referrals you might need to request. As always, networking is key.

What will you leverage or invest to obtain it?

Let me share this piece of wisdom that I've learned: everything you will ever want to accomplish in this life requires a sacrifice and investment from you personally. I was talking with a friend the other day, and we spoke about Beyoncé. As amazing as her career is, she has sacrificed her childhood, anonymity, and ability to just be without being affected by any opinions from the public—and that's tough, even for someone with such fame and success. Everything in life that's worth something comes with a price. The idea here is to know what that sacrifice is, and for you to resolve that you're okay with that investment.

How hard are you willing to work?

One of the primary keys to entrepreneurship is your strength. You need to consider how hard you'll work for what you want. *Shark Tank* investor Mark Cuban once said, "To be a successful entrepreneur, for a period of time, you have to be myopic and run with blinders on and remain incredibly focused, and once you have reached the desired level of success, then maintain it." This level of devotion requires an inner drive that I think you might have already. I find that those who are successful in this business work hard and enjoy this level of devotion.

How will you share it with the world?

As an entrepreneur, you don't just create a business solely for yourself: you create it for other people. Being an entrepreneur is about how you can package and monetize your idea for the world.

In conclusion, now that you have those key questions, I'm going to go into two primary attributes you also need to possess to be a successful entrepreneur: personal accountability and the ability to multitask.

PERSONAL ACCOUNTABILITY

To be an entrepreneur, you have to be personally accountable to yourself, as well as your goals and visions. To this end, I recommend doing a weekly honesty audit, which encompasses constant self-reflection and evaluation so that, moving forward, you can keep going with what works, and change what doesn't! Some questions for your weekly review:

- What went well?
- What do I want to be recognized for?
- What can I celebrate?

- Where did I drop the ball?
- What can I do better next week?

THE ABILITY TO SUCCEED AT THE ART OF MULTI-TASKING

To be a musician, especially when you pursue it as a profession, you have to learn how to multi-task in the midst of your pursuit. You learn to make a singular choice to sing or play an instrument, but if you seek to have a private instructor, he or she is going to advise you to work on multiple things at the same time, yet with one focus.

As a working musician, you will have to develop multiple relationships with employers and entities to make sure that you are able to make a successful living. I mention this because some ask the question, "If I am a musician, why should I even be worried about entrepreneurship and branding?"

I challenge you with the question, "How can you not be?" To be a talented musician means that you are an individual who shows up to the room with a talent in hand. However, your entrepreneurial abilities are what will determine how far you go within that room, and potentially beyond the room.

One of my great friends is a talented musician with several successful businesses in the area of real estate and commercial development. I asked him how he fostered the ability to learn to be great in those other areas. He responded, "Ulysses, when you learn to become a great musician, everything else is easy after that."

I think it's important to study the power of multi-tasking and to learn how to be impactful in several areas to get yourself to where it is that you desire to go ultimately in your career.

Reflections for thought and discussion:

1. What makes you entrepreneurial? What do you need to work on?
2. What are you willing to sacrifice to attain your goals?

3. How hard are you willing to work?
4. What types of self-reflection do you do?

Reflections for writing:

1. Do you currently multi-task? Write at least three examples of what you currently do—or what you could do, if you're not currently multi-tasking.
2. Write some examples of how you are personally accountable. Start by examining what you did this week, as suggested in this chapter. Write the answers to the following questions:
   - What went well?
   - What do I want to be recognized for?
   - What can I celebrate?
   - Where did I drop the ball?
   - What can I do better next week?

CHAPTER 11

Learning to Sell Yourself: Public Speaking, Writing, and Meetings

"I'm not a businessman, I am a business, man."—Jay-Z, Rapper, Songwriter, Producer, Entrepreneur, and Record Executive

Part of succeeding in the music business depends on your ability to recognize all these components that we're mentioning here. You will need to be many things—including a business. As Jay-Z says about himself, you need to be your business!

As a musician, your reputation is secured by the work you do daily. You need to constantly strive to understand many aspects of the industry, as well as the different people and roles you have to deal with. Therefore, it's necessary for you to see yourself as a business, and even an empire, so the decisions that you make are strategic—like a business's.

Part of this—becoming a successful business—means you have to develop a skill set that you may not have had before. For example, in my case, I had to learn how to truly sell myself, without doing it in a shameless or degrading way (that was my fear). I had to learn how to be bold about my talent and unafraid to push myself to a certain level to get the results I desired.

Let me be more specific: I needed to learn how to clearly articulate my vision, thoughts, and overall goals to potential investors in my talent and business ideas. Part of this, as I'll explain momentarily, was learning how to be a good public speaker. Now, I know that some of you are cringing at this idea. But, dear students, this is a key part of the process.

PUBLIC SPEAKING

Years ago, my mother would always say to me, "You have to learn to stop being shy, because while you're being shy, someone else is taking your opportunities. So, get over yourself!"

In my case, this was easier said than done. I was not a natural in this area. I spent years working on this very important skill. I'll tell you a bit about my process.

Finding models

I started by studying great speakers and orators. I would listen to their speeches and pay attention to their usage of words, their inflection, their rate of speaking, their tone, and their use of pauses. Often, I'd play their talks over and over, and then try my best to emulate their techniques—which, by the way, is not totally different from listening to the jazz musicians I admire!

Recording my voice—and my message

I remember the first time I heard my voice on tape, it was dreadful. I'm sure some of you who have done this exercise can understand both my initial reluctance and then that scary feeling of, "This is what I sound like when I talk?"

But I started learning how to tolerate how I sounded, and ultimately how to make myself become better at speaking. I started monitoring my own speaking skill by paying attention to the words I chose, those I needed to better articulate, and my ability to incorporate different elements so that my speaking could be clearer—and more effective.

I also started working on "getting to the point." After all, as artists, we all have to learn how to sell our ideas, and also not take all day figuring out how to sell them. We need to reach what we want to say in a relatively short amount of time.

How can you improve your skills? Well, in addition to listening and practicing, there are multiple programs like Toastmasters, or even workshops through schools—like public speaking classes—and exercises that can help increase your comfort in this area.

CONSIDERATION OF AUDIENCE

It's not just how you speak that's important; it's also key to recognize whom you'll be addressing. In fact, your "audience" can be quite diverse, ranging from potential clients and investors to fans. And just like you don't talk to your family members in the same way you might address a professor, you need to learn how to shift your speaking. In some ways, we could say you need to custom-design your speaking so that you can move the relevant agenda forward. Here I'm sharing some examples of audiences, and how to tailor your talking. In all cases, you need to do your homework so that you are better prepared; this is NOT something you should wing.

A potential client

People who you desire to invest in you need your true interest in them, not their wallet. When speaking to a potential client, I find that you have to really understand more about them than about your desires for them. Figure out how to tap into their world. Try to discover their interests and connect them to the world that you want to bring them into. Try to find conversational points that are not all about you—or what you want. People can feel that pure energy, and they'll want to give more to you when they realize that you are just interested in them. In my case, I feel so honored just to know any of the donors or mentors I have in my life, and if you feel the same—and show it—you'll win them over.

An investor

All investors are serious about their money and maintaining their wealth, and they want to give to something that will grow. Prior to speaking with an investor, put yourself in their shoes: What are you willing to write a check for? Treat an investor the same way you desire someone to treat you.

With all potential investors, I make sure that I have a package full of data that includes the following: who I am, what I have accomplished, and demonstrations of both. Having my "track record" on hand helps so that they can see what I have been able to do with money before they even came to the table. Investors want to see that other people have and are willing to invest in you. They want to join the party, not start it; very rarely will you meet someone who wants to be the first investor in your business. Make sure that what you desire them to invest in is something that's growing, and has the potential to grow more.

An audience

As a performer, learning how to communicate with an audience is something you must hone. Again, being talented is not enough. There are so many musicians and creatives out here in the world who can overwhelm you with their talent but cannot maintain that feeling with their stage banter. I have always been thankful that I found my voice with audiences pretty early, and have been able to know how to speak to them. Much of that comes from my desire and ability to reach them, and understand them. Find your voice; don't try to be something you aren't. I remember when I joined Christian McBride's various bands, it was the first time I heard someone speak whose style and approach I admired. It's very natural, and comes genuinely from his personality. You need to find YOUR voice and use it to communicate with your fans. This is a process, for some, but I promise—once you get it, you don't lose it. It just keeps getting better.

Designing and delivering a set to an audience

I was traveling with Christian Sands and Luques Curtis, two dynamic musicians within my generation, and we were speaking about the power of being able to build a set list for an audience. I build my set list, or at least the framework of it, weeks before my shows. I think about the audience, and I imagine the feeling they will have and what I want them to experience from my shows. I really think about the whole experience as an arc. It starts by imagining their entrance—and what they might, emotionally, walk in the door with. The arc continues as I create a list of music that will take them on a journey that will keep them engaged. Finally, I consider how I want them to leave; I want to leave them with a sweet taste and remembrance of the show. It's important for performing artists to consider the entirety of the audience's experience, and build a setlist for a show with that reality in mind.

Promoters

In that same conversation with Luques and Christian, we also talked about our mentors, Mulgrew Miller, Donald Harrison, and Dr. Billy Taylor, and how they taught us how to deal with promoters in this business. Promoters are the money men and women that make shows and tours possible. It's helpful to have a great relationship with them, with a large respectful component, because they're the ones who truly make it possible for you to make money with your art. As a musician, never overstep your position as a sideman and create dialogue with the promoter in a way that makes them uncomfortable. Be very conscious of your conversations with the promoter. This is when you need to adopt your businessperson persona; you can be friendly and respectful, but you and your promoter need to maintain a business relationship first and foremost.

Believe me, dear students, here again I speak from personal experience. Early in the business, I spent a lot of time trying to befriend promoters because I eventually wanted to be able to bring my own projects to them, and I thought that this—becoming pals with them—was the way. But my objective became twisted and backfired; it came across as desperate and sometimes disrespectful to the bandleaders who hired me. Again, learning to be a businessperson who is friendly and respectful is of the utmost importance in most of your professional relationships.

Bandleaders

Bandleaders, like promoters, merit your respect first and foremost. After all, this is the person who is juggling so much and navigating a great deal so that you—and your band—can succeed. You are in *their* band, and need to consistently and constantly keep this in mind. How do you do this? Well, in my case, I go for the service mode: as soon as I am with the bandleader, I figure out any ways that I can help this person attain his or her goals, which, ultimately, will also help me.

MEETINGS—A.K.A. SITUATIONAL AUDIENCES

Now, dear students, we move into a slightly different type of audience interaction: meetings. This actually involves a lot of the points mentioned previously, but the goal is often different.

Meetings, whether in person or on the phone, are vital when you are an entrepreneur. In fact, in many cases your ability to navigate meetings will determine how successful you will be in your entrepreneurial endeavors.

Meetings in the music industry serve a myriad of purposes:

- Get to know the parties that may be collaborating;
- Plant the seed for a new idea;
- Gain more information about an idea;
- Flush out the logistics of executing the idea;
- Ultimately move the process forward so the idea can be realized.

In all of these situations, chances are they'll involve someone's consideration of you as an artist for a particular opportunity. If the objective is to decide whether or not someone is going to invest in you, or grant you an opportunity to move forward with an endeavor, then the impression you give—as I'm sure you recognize—can make or break the deal.

So, your goal, in this case, is to close the deal: you want to convince the potential client that you're the one. I like to call these opportunities "closing moments." When you think about a closing (when buying a home), it symbolizes concluding and making the deal happen and coming to a close. Being a closer is being the person who has a clear agenda, someone who knows how to show up to meetings to clearly communicate to all parties with the goal of mutual success. Being a good closer means that you are someone who can gracefully finalize a win-win situation. But before we talk about closing, let's step back for a bit, and talk about opening—and preparation.

THE OPENING

Your start is as important as your closing! You want to "hook" your listener in from the beginning by setting the scene. An good opener plants the seed—whether it's formal or informal—of the direction that everything will go.

But even before opening, there's a lot of prep to be done.

PREPARATION CONSIDERATIONS

Especially when you're not as comfortable at public speaking yet—and even when you are—it's important to have your ideas, and focus, in front of you. One way to do this is to outline the following—and by outline, I mean that my suggestion is to write this all down.

Make sure your objectives are clear!

Make sure your mission is clear. This is for two reasons: if you're nervous, you could "stray" and get away from the point, and subsequently, your audience won't be able to follow. Here's an idea: write out a kind of speech. Then work backwards and write down your key points. These points will clearly give you your agenda for the meeting. Make sure that, before the meeting, you have sent the client all the necessary information that they need to know about you or your opportunity. Leave very little to question for them, which will leave room for them to say no, or postpone their yes.

Consider who's going to be in the room— and consider them!

Again, this goes back to audience: it's critical that you know who the players will be in a meeting—and, thanks to the Internet, this shouldn't be too tough to do. Whether it's a one-on-one or a conference of several, get a list of attendees and Google each one. Check out their LinkedIn profiles and/or their Facebook pages to try to gain insights as to who they are and what they're bringing to the table.

Think about what obstacles could occur— and be prepared to remove them!

Depending on who's in the room, and what your objectives are, there could be predictable obstacles that would steer your meeting in a direction not of your choosing. Think about what those might be, and how you might counter them. Identify potential issues, and try to resolve them even prior to the meeting.

Decide on your ideal outcome—but be flexible!

If you've sent your agenda, and all are clear regarding the objective and level of importance of the meeting, then the next step is helping the attendees see the "big picture" of the meeting. You need to keep everything connected to the theme—and focused. However, something may come up that you didn't anticipate. Listen. Be humble. And be flexible.

Be personable, direct, and appreciative— and know when it's time to finish!

There's a reason that people say, "time is money!" Now, I'm not telling you to talk fast; I'm telling you to be aware of the folks in the room, and just like when you're performing, you need to be able to "read" the room. Get to your point, and hold it there. Conclude when appropriate—and make sure it's timely. I'll get to body language in a moment.

Body language: What are you saying—and what are they saying, with and without words?

I find that I can tell how a person feels about the opportunity or matter that they want to discuss based on their body language—and this is something that you'd greatly benefit from learning. It may even be timely to do some research on body language cues so you can pick up on subtle signals that the person or client may be sending you about their interest in helping you with this opportunity or not. This will be a big helpful factor in guiding you to read the room.

A FEW ADDITIONAL POINTS

Behavior in a meeting is also crucial. Your ability to be professional is of the utmost importance. What is being professional? Making eye contact, not looking at your phone, not yawning. Listen, and be your best you. Be more formal than informal. Yes, behavior, like body language, can be read—and misread. Sit up straight (but not so that you're visibly uncomfortable!) and pay attention. If you don't, it can be disarming and distract from the success of the meeting.

Location can also be instrumental. You want to be in the right place for the right client, whose needs should be first and foremost. It could be an office meeting or perhaps one over lunch, dinner, drinks, or even on the golf course; the choices are numerous. You have to really think about the position the person is in, what would make them feel comfortable, and even how much time they have.

In my case, if the person is someone that I really need something from, I want the meeting to be convenient—not difficult—for them. I will therefore often ask them to choose a place, one that requires minimal effort on their part. Doing the opposite, like making someone travel or creating a difficult location/time, is a quick way to lose a potential opportunity.

One last but equally important meeting consideration is to make sure the signals are clear. For example, the hour of the day, and the location, and certain environments, can send messages you might not intend. As a producer, it's so comfortable for me to have meetings at my home because all of my resources are there. However, I had to start altering that because merely suggesting my home sent mixed signals to certain clients. Dating and meetings are two totally different realms, and I try to keep them very far apart—and suggest the same to you. Here, as in most cases, communication is key. It's important to make sure everyone is comfortable, and being clear about the matter and goals is key to ensuring success.

LET'S NOW GO BACK TO THE CLOSING

Your closing is your chance to do the following:

1. **Thank the participants.** This is when you humbly address everyone there and show your appreciation for both their effort and attendance.
2. **Summarize** the key points of the meeting. You can do this by going over the agenda and reiterating the objectives.
3. **Briefly address next steps**: If there are action items, restate them.
4. **Leave something behind**: Whether it's a CD, a folder of articles, or a sweet, leave something that shows that you are who you are! You want them, after all, to remember you in the most positive light.

Once you leave the meeting, you'll want to think about follow-up. No matter what the decision, you'll want to show your gratitude for the time the participants spent considering your idea/proposal—or whatever it is. Promptly send a follow-up note, ideally an email, thanking the guests for their attendance, and also announcing next steps.

AND—IF AT FIRST YOU DON'T SUCCEED . . . KEEP TRYING!

As a jazz musician, I am constantly challenged to improvise and create ideas in every measure, and every bar of a tune. The goal is to play the melody, the form, but then figure out new ways to stretch the melody, or alter it with inspiration. Jazz musicians constantly want to make ideas new and fresh. Mulgrew Miller, my mentor, used to tell me, "Ulysses, my goal every night on stage is to play something I have never heard from me before."

I translate this thinking into other aspects of living. Much of my life and focus daily is reaching for and attaining those moments, and I seek to add that philosophy—about keeping it new and fresh and full of ideas—to my endeavors within the world of entrepreneurship. My mother and I always say that if you put us in a room with a blank sheet of paper, we would walk out with a business on the paper, knowing all the necessary steps and people to talk to bring that idea to fruition. When we created our nonprofit, Don't Miss a Beat, we sat at that very kitchen table in my parents' house, and we focused in on this idea, and then the business structure and plan of the idea, the target audience, and the first steps that we needed to take to make it happen.

REMEMBER TO BE YOU—AND TELL YOUR STORY!

Yes, I've given you a lot to consider about how you should behave in certain situations, but dear students, remember that this is not at the expense of losing you. It's important to always remember: no one can be better at being you than **you**.

I remember meeting a student recently, and when this student played for me in the lesson, he sounded very much like a famous musician. I began to ask him where he was from, and what his village sounded like. He began to play the *sound* of his hometown, and I was moved to tears.

He noticed this, stopped playing, looked at me and smiled. I told him, "Never forget, in your moment of pursuing greatness musically, your story."

After all, we have all been given an authentic journey and story. Out of the billions of individuals who exist on this planet, only we can authentically be ourselves. When speaking publicly, or in meeting with people to pitch an idea that you may have, don't remove your journey or that authentic piece of the puzzle that makes you who you are. That's what will make people invest in you fully. As Mulgrew Miller told me years ago, "There is always room for you."

The more I became comfortable with my truth and story, the more it drew people into a position in which they wanted to know more about me. This, wanting to get to know you for you, the whole package of you, is ultimately your goal in this business.

Reflections for thought and discussion:

1. What's *your business*? How would you explain it to someone?
2. Are you comfortable speaking to others? What areas should you work on?
3. Do you see yourself more as a meeting opener or closer? Support your statement with examples.
4. What makes "your story" a unique one?

Reflections for writing:

1. Imagine you are meeting a potential client. Write three reasons why they should invest in you, and record yourself "selling" yourself to this client.
2. Listen to your recording, and write down five areas for improvement.
3. Who are three people whose projects you admire? Write down their names, and the specific projects.
4. What are at least three of your own projects you'd like to bring to fruition? Write down notes as to how you would sell each one.

CHAPTER 12

Marketing: Branding, Communication, and Social Media

In Chapter 11, I talked about how you should sell yourself in a meeting, and about the art of public speaking and how that is something you need to be able to do—and, ideally, master. This skill involves being able to adjust yourself to different audiences. Well, dear students, marketing is also all about adjusting yourself to different audiences—but on a larger scale!

Marketing, by definition, is the promotion of a product or resource. As artists, we are constantly selling ourselves and figuring out how to promote or present ourselves in order to gain the larger marketplace.

According to the book *The 22 Immutable Laws of Marketing* by Al Ries and Jack Trout, "Marketing is a battle of ideas. If you are going to succeed, you must have an idea or attribute of your own to focus your efforts around."

This quote resonates loudly with me, which is why I'm passing it along to you. I had no idea how important it would be for artists to be their own marketing team, to constantly and consistently work with their own marketing agenda and strategy. Since it is often challenging to change a mind once it's made up, or convince someone they should "need" or "want" something that they don't currently possess, your marketing efforts have to be devoted to using ideas and concepts that might already be there—and making a bridge. You have to connect with people's minds on a level that attracts them to whatever it is you're wanting them to listen to, and, ultimately, purchase.

In the realm of developing a kind of selling campaign, sometimes people lean too far into the obvious. Dear students, I'm trying to steer you away from that. So, what is the obvious? Well, I'm saying obvious in the sense that it's been done. Let me explain: so many students come to me with ideas that they perceive as unique. However, upon further discussion or examination, they realize that, unfortunately, their idea is not unique; the idea has been pitched on numerous occasions.

However, and thankfully, that's not the only case. In fact, there are one-of-a-kind ideas that come by me from time to time—and that is when I get excited. This often happens when people look within themselves and come up with unique combinations of their talent, resources, and wisdom to create a pitch or project that is unlike any-thing else. That, in my opinion, is gold in the marketing world.

Here I'm presenting for marketing those ideas that I think are most relevant to you. We'll also dive deeper into the realm that is especially key in one prevalent and oh-so-valuable area: social media.

Let's move in with the continuation of a key theme for all of us artists: the audience.

CATER TO YOUR AUDIENCE

Again, you need to define who your audience is, and listen to those whom you're trying to reach.

I remember listening to an amazing story one day on a podcast about a marketing genius, Tom Burrell, who was the first African-American man to represent the voice of people of color to ad agencies. He created numerous campaigns for larger corporations that spoke in a very specific ways to the community.

For example, there was one advertisement in particular that I remember. It was for McDonald's, which was—back then—one of the first corporations to take the risk of focusing and entire ad campaign on that African-American community. The ad portrays a young man in Chicago who gets his first job in McDonald's. As his journey continues, he begins to positively transform his life by working his way up in McDonald's through various positions, while also going to college, and making a positive impact in our community. What did this show? It showed a young African-American man not only making a positive impact in his community, but also succeeding in his personal life. This advertisement apparently spoke to many: it completely shifted mindsets and contributed to the increase in sales for McDonald's within the community.

I share this to illustrate that we should take the time to find more definition and focus as far as our audiences. We need to find out who is into what we do—or potentially into—and reach out to them. A manager said to me one time, "Ulysses, stop worrying about everyone that's into what you do. Find those that are already convinced of who you are and give consistently to them and that group of folks will eventually expand."

This moved me, because I think we as creatives are many times chasing our tails, and even at times exhausting ourselves trying to tell the world about who we are, when in fact we'll never reach everyone. It's important to nurture the fans and believers in what we do. How do we do this? We need to understand that as we cater to them, they will invite others into that journey.

THE LAW OF LEADERSHIP

I learned a lot about marketing from not only personal experience, but also from several books, including the one I mentioned earlier: *The 22 Immutable Laws of Marketing.*

One of the points the authors make, under their "The Law of Leadership," section, is that the best step in marketing is to be the first at something. In doing so, the book states—and I agree—that you'll get the attention of people. If you can create the impression of being number one, the sky's the limit as far as your marketing potential! Obviously, there are so many other considerations around this truth, but being unique in a field is a huge boost.

I remember being on tour in St. Lucia and I met a guy who had a backline company, which I spoke about earlier, and his advice still stays with me. He said, "Ulysses, choose a business idea that solves a problem." He told me about his background: he was a musician, like all of us, and spending a great deal of time on the road. When his wife got pregnant, he wanted to figure out a way to raise his family and be more present at home. Then he had an idea: he looked at his own musical instrument collection, and started building on it. He found various resources, including pawn shops, and started supplying instruments for various shows around town. He soon developed a reputation for having great gear—and exactly what musicians needed. Today his company still supplies backline for some of the top music festivals in the world. As he said, once you use your talent to solve a problem, you'll never not be successful.

BRANDING

Branding is another area that musicians need to grasp. Just as we talked about you thinking of yourself as a business, when you see yourself as a brand, you make different decisions. Let's talk about this for a bit.

Your brand can expand, but it must be presented in a way that doesn't misrepresent you—or confuse people. I remember having a conversation with Andre Kimo Stone Guess, Career Architect, who runs GuessWorks, an artist management and music production firm, and who also manages many of the great talents in jazz.

We had breakfast one day on the road, and he told me that I had a lot of great ideas, but that I needed to be careful not to expose all of them to the same audience. He pointed out that on my current website, I was doing too much: I was advertising my production company, and more, while also talking about my career as a drummer. He explained that if someone really wanted to hire me as a drummer, they would get distracted by all of the other things I was promoting.

Andre suggested that I keep doing everything, but that I work to categorize it differently. He suggested developing other, more focused websites to showcase my different areas of work, so that potential clients—and my audience—could be directed accordingly.

So, dear students, keep doing what you're doing, but try to keep it focused.

And speaking of branding and coming from a successful place, you want to create a logo that also clearly represents you. My advice? Keep it simple and representative. This is certainly easier said than done. Many times, I see young companies create logos that are overdone, or don't have the clarity or connection to the brand. In my experience, my own logo over the years has gone through many revisions and alterations based on the various businesses I have worked with. You need to find the right graphic designer, and make sure the logo quality and files match both your website and any of the documents that it will be printed on.

SOCIAL MEDIA

"Activate your fans, don't just collect them like baseball cards."—Jay Baer, Writer and Business Strategist

We can't talk about branding and marketing without getting into social media. According to statistics from Wikipedia and others, there are approximately 7.7 billion people in the world. According to Facebook, 2.5 billion regularly log on—or at least did at the end of 2019. This number is huge for any artist—or anyone who wants to reach a large chunk of people. Today, you have more access to the public through your phone and laptop than you might in your immediate world, meaning next door or in your entire city.

The impact of art has always been measured through the masses of people who are influenced by the work, and given the huge level of access that we are given to people globally, social media has a starring role. For this reason, record labels, agencies, production companies, and studios look to leverage the influence an artist has by virtue of his or her followers. And, in fact, that number can be wielded as part of the negotiation for the level of deal you could be contracted for.

Many different artists, especially from generations that came before me, have sought to discredit or even ignore social media, but it's already become a standard rule that if you don't exist on social media, you don't exist at all. This is no trend; it is part of the industry standard.

There has never before been a moment in time when a single artist, just by using a few devices, has access to the world at large for free, with the only limiting factor being how creative one can be. Aside from having followers, branding is possible thanks to social media on a whole different level. It gives you—the artist—complete power. Social media allows you to create, have access to your current fan base, *and* expand it daily. It's important that you are giving your followers something substantive and not just playing a game of "please pay attention to me."

When I was lecturing at Stanford University, so many of the students asked the question, "How do you remain authentic on social media?" My response was simple: be honest about your life. If there is something that you are experiencing, and you want to share it, that's cool. If it's something that is not what you want to share, don't share it with the public. (I'll touch on TMI in a bit!) The goal I feel with social media is that, before you begin engaging on there, you should decide what are you willing for people to know and not know. It's important to be yourself and not compare your journey and life to others, since that's when things can get really dangerous.

Let's bring this back into the context of this book and what it means: you have to approach your social media profile from the perspective of a business, not your personal opinion about how you want to be viewed. Obviously, there are some occupations where it might not matter as much if you have a presence online. However, in the case of us artists and creatives, it matters! Building and maintaining a substantial following will help us in multiple ways. Furthermore, it's important to note that so much positively is possible with social media, and you can really use it to do some great things and make moves.

First let's determine what approach you might apply to your communication on social media.

THREE TYPES OF COMMUNICATION ON SOCIAL MEDIA

I have created these three different categories of users based on my research by being an avid social media explorer and how it affects my own businesses as well.

Completely professional

This type of social media user expresses only speaks—or shares—information about professional matters consistently. These people spend most of their social media time with the focus of professional companies and people viewing it.

80/20 professional mostly with a hint of personal expression

This user expresses what I feel is a nice balance between having a purpose online, but still while keeping people safely engaged with their humanity. This is the category I fall into, where I express a certain amount of professionalism because it's what so much of my life is focused on. However, it's nice to occasionally let people into the world of your personal life. Sometimes I'll share a "scene" from a performance, or a snippet of me practicing, along with some relevant words of wisdom and encouragement; this is a natural extension of my personality. I play, and I encourage. And though I touch on some private thoughts, I should add that most of the time, those who are really close to me, I hold very dear to me. When I am with them, I work on being fully present and in the moment, which means there is very little social media traction during that time.

Completely personal

This type of social media user expresses what I feel is a ticking time bomb, and essentially could ruin their careers with one tweet, post, or snapchat. Recently in the news, there have been several individuals who have used their social media to promote racist and negative political mindsets, which everyone is within their right to feel. However, you should not express them publicly. When their jobs discovered their political and racial thoughts, they fired them.

Some students had their college acceptances rescinded because of it. In this day and age, no one wants their brand associated publicly with someone who thinks and speaks negatively towards others. So just be really cautious about what you put out there. Before you post it, think, "Is this something I would put out on a billboard for anyone and everyone to see?" If the answer is no, well, then, there you have it.

Let's move on to one of the most defining aspects of using social media: number of followers.

As I stated earlier, followers matter—in a big way. I was on the road a few weeks ago and I ran into a very dear friend of mine who works for a very prominent PR company in the world of jazz. We had a very enlightening conversation around the topic of the importance of social media today.

She was saying to me that publications, labels, and even certain award shows are measuring their interest in artists based on their social media following. They've even identified a number of followers that someone has to have prior to being considered for certain opportunities.

In light of this, you may be considering ways that you can make these numbers happen. My opinion is that it should happen more organically. Based on my philosophy, I've collected my rules for social media engagement:

Do not purchase additional followers.

I think that people need to build their following the old-fashioned way: brick by brick. How can you do this? By being creative. If you don't have that many followers, chances are there is something about your profile, personality, or communication that is not engaging.

Do not adopt a trend to try to gain followers.

Again, if you're just trying to find easy engagement, your followers will catch on fast. Inspire using the tools you have: your talent and cleverness. This is the way you can appeal to others.

Present the real you, and it will attract admirers and followers of your brand and talent.

People will react to you if it's the real you. Think of yourself as a business, identify what defines you, and build on that.

Give yourself time to build your following.

I remember when I realized that based on my future goals, I needed to start engaging more on social media, my numbers were really low. However, I met with a friend of mine, a social media guru, who encouraged me to utilize key components of my career and life and engage with others online. I looked at my life, and figured out what were the coolest things to me about what I get to do, and one of them is travel. I thought to myself, "How many people get to see a different city several times a week?" I decided that I could show something—through photos, videos, and narratives—that most people don't get to see. My followers subsequently increased. Of course, there is still more I can do as far as learning how to monetize and grow the following more.

I view social media as another aspect of my career that I have to work on and develop. After all, as I'm sharing with you here, just as in your case, it's also integral to my gaining more exposure.

Consult with a professional who not only has the experience but also the results and proof on his or her page.

Right now, there are many people who are calling themselves influencers, and they don't have a large following. So, if someone is trying to sell him or herself to you, check out their page—and track record. The person that I asked for help from not only has a large following, but also gets paid by large corporations to run their social media programs and keep their approach on the cutting edge of what will allow them to continuously grow. Look for someone with savvy and experience, not just someone who talks a big game.

ALL PROFILES ARE NOT CREATED EQUAL

It's important to know that though some people may be popular by virtue of a public position they're in, not everyone's profile will garner a large amount of attention. For instance, some of my friends who are actors, if they're lucky enough to get a job with a hit show that appears in the home of millions of people, will get huge followings—just by virtue of being in that position. Obviously, this is a special situation. In my case, I don't compare myself to them, or anyone. That being said, it's great to look at other people's social profiles as a point of reference, or for ways you can grow and adjust your profile. However, do not compare and contrast or "remold" yourself based on someone else. Everyone has a unique story that gives them the ability to engage in their way. You just need to find yours! How do you do that?

It's important to spend time really analyzing what's special about you and your story, and then promote and build an audience around that.

HOW MANY FOLLOWERS DO I NEED?

This, dear students, is the big question. I remember meeting with a record label, and they were very interested in me musically. However, at the time, I had less than 7,500 followers, and as much as they were interested, they stated that they didn't sign artists who had less than 10,000 followers. I have my own opinions about the validity of that whole matter, but this is their truth, and companies need some guarantee on how they can monetize their investment in you. Knowing that you have reach and influence over a certain number of people gives them a guarantee of potential return on investment. This goes back to the point I stated earlier: followers are crucial.

Recently, I questioned a PR person, who advised that for certain opportunities, you need 20,000 followers or more. The reality is that some of you reading this book can work all day and all night to try to up your numbers. But no matter what you do, there is going to be a limit on the amount of followers you will gain. Why? Just as in the example of a TV actor, this is because some people's life and careers invite a lot of attention, while others don't.

Let me tell you a bit of what I did—and what worked.

What I have constantly done, when I had 100 followers, or now, when I have amassed more of a following, is try to focus in on solid content and give your followers something beyond just a cute photo, or a video of your performing. There are people who are on social media all day and all night; I want people to feel that my social profile is linked to my real profile, and that they can gain something substantive from my social media accounts.

Again, as I've mentioned, I've looked around and investigated this area—as I'm guessing you have as well. Like you, I find there are people who literally operate their social media platforms on shock value. Once I heard a celebrity ask the question, "What are we giving those that follow us?" It's an honest question, and one that I keep in mind. So here's my advice: don't just focus on quantity, because there are sites you can go to, and checks that you can write that can make that possible very quickly. Sincerity, I believe, shines through: you can tell who has real influence and who doesn't.

INFLUENCERS

When we talk about followers, we can't ignore the area of influencers—people who have such huge followings that they've established a kind of credibility in particular industries. This is a relatively new area—and one that is strong alternative to traditional promotion and advertising. Many companies/advertisers, as you may already know, use influencers to reach an audience that they cannot otherwise reach.

Now, getting back to you, not everyone is going to be a social media influencer; this is the truth, and I feel the sooner we come to terms with that, the quicker we'll have more of an authentic page. Several of my friends who have more followers than I do have made certain career choices that make that a reality:

- They may work for an employer that allows them to tour larger audiences;

- They make music that reaches masses, versus my operating in mostly niche markets musically;
- They are simply more popular than I am; and/or
- They are better and more engaged at social media than I am.

I've accepted this as a reality—no matter what the reason, I don't take this personally. I can tell you that through the years, I've noticed in my own world that there are posts that may earn many likes, and ones that may get half as many. However, I also see that the amount of followers on my accounts is constantly increasing, and I focus more on that than one particular post. I just try to make sure that all of my posts are authentic and organic.

Does it bother me that my numbers haven't skyrocketed? No! I've learned to recognize that it's not a flaw, and to use that information wisely. This continues to prompt me to develop my true audience. In your case, I encourage you—as always—to do your homework: study your favorite social media influencers and learn from them. This doesn't mean you need to copy them. Again, find your own voice in that realm. One other key point: social media also is not fair game for everyone; I have seen mentors who have careers that are amazing and rewarding careers but it hasn't translated to social media because they simply don't deem it as important to their careers.

OTHER IMPORTANT SOCIAL MEDIA POINTS FOR YOU TO CONSIDER: T.M.I. (TOO MUCH INFORMATION)

Social media is a way to engage with the world, but it's important to understand the world has access to your social media. Knowing what you had for dinner, or how sick you are feeling at the moment, or about intimate moments with loved ones is, is in my opinion, private information. In my case, I say that you can have full access to my art, but not full access to me. I have to keep myself separate from the art, because otherwise my entire life is lived in the public, and that's not fair to me, nor to those I love. Some things and moments in my life need to remain sacred.

When we give those moments to the world, we cannot take them back. I say this to remind you, dear students, that if you are building a business, you should be careful about showing too much. Based on my experience with students, and just from perusing the Internet in general, I have to say that I believe too many of us put too much of our personal business out into the world. As artists, I think we need to still have a level of discretion in our lives.

As you embark on this next phase of your career, I ask you to consider this point carefully: proceed on the social media front with caution.

SOCIAL MEDIA DOS

Okay—we've touched on several don'ts; let's go back to dos. Here are things you should do/consider as you develop your online persona:

Do the Google test

If you're going to examine your presence, and I encourage you to do so, then one thing I highly recommend is to Google yourself, and note that your social media stats appear in your Google search. Obviously, this is what anyone else—like an employer, for example—sees too, which means that for most employers, when they Google you (and most of them do), anything that is only your social media channels will pop up; and they will utilize that as part of their consideration process towards you for an opportunity.

Create a username that can help people find you

I see many artists who want to draw many people to their page and career, yet they create alter ego names and make it difficult for potential followers to find them. If you've done this, created pages under different names when you want yours to grow, you should consider combining them. Create a user name that easily links to you.

Be cognizant of the photos you choose

My friend, Africa Miranda, a wonderful model and beautypreneur, gave me some great advice related to photos. We sat down for an informal meeting one day and, since she has a large online presence, I started asking her about social media. She checked out my presence there, and said "Ulysses, your career and life are really cool, but your images are not on the level of your career."

When I asked her, just to confirm, if I should have someone take some better photos, she responded with a loud, "Yes!"

And so, I listened to her! I started making sure my images were consistently better. Again, dear students, this is part of thinking and acting like a business. What happened after I changed my photos? My following shot up. Additionally, I started to get approached by various photographers who wanted to shoot me to add new types of photos to my profile.

Add video

Videos—and the quality of videos—are just as important. Adrian Ross, who has been my PR agent for various projects the last few years, also pulled my coattail about adding video content to my page. I disagreed with him at first because, quite frankly, I felt that pictures were enough to manage, and his asking me to add videos to the list of things I need to create seemed like a lot of work for little return. But, well, I was wrong: videos have been very helpful because they gave me a different way to engage with my audience. Great still images are helpful, but video allows, especially in the case of musicians, to invite people into a world that they may never otherwise get to see up close and personal.

Monetize your social media

I have several friends who are social media influencers, and because of their brand influence and reach, they are able to get support and even fees to talk about various brands within their own brand. As I mentioned in the section on endorsements, I have, thankfully, long enjoyed the support of musical companies alongside of my brand. Just now I'm getting to the point where I have been approached by additional companies and offered nominal fees to speak publicly about theirs on my profile, and can seek out additional partnerships with companies whose products can help me. In doing so, I develop relationships that are mutually beneficial.

In terms of your ability, there are multiple ways you can monetize your own social media profile, either directly or in addition. Though larger companies are tougher to approach without an agent, there are a lot of smaller or startup companies who may be looking for artists to represent them. There are definitely dollars that can be made on social media with your influence—if, again, you have the right number of followers.

However, as in every point I've raised, your work in social media—and your potential success there—requires forethought, work, and consistency.

Reflections for thought and discussion:
1. What idea or attribute do you have that could be focused on through marketing?
2. What kind of social media presence do you currently have?
3. Look over your posts on social media. How could they be improved?
4. After reading this chapter, what about that presence might you change?
5. Google yourself. What did you find? What does this mean?

Reflections for writing:
1. Assess your marketing strategy. What can you do to improve it? Write down several ideas.
2. Create a strategy for your online presence. Write down three creative ways you can enhance your brand and vision on your social media platform.
3. Develop a holistic marketing timeline that starts immediately (what you can do today) and bring it into the next three months. Write down dates and plans relevant to your

own marketing, and keeping in mind points presented here in this chapter and previously:

- What you can do TODAY:
- What you can do next week:
- What you can do in two weeks:
- What you can do next month:
- What you can do in two months:
- What you can do in three months:

PART IV

ART & SURVIVAL

Art, in all of its expressions, doesn't intrinsically translate into survival. However, armed with a wealth of business-relevant information, this section brings you as an artist—and a business—back to fundamental basics. Art & Survival is about the merging of these two different but interconnected areas. This section is designed to motivate and educate you as it takes you into the mindset of personal—artistic and professional—success.

CHAPTER 13

Protection of Yourself and Your Art

It's important not just to focus on creating art but how you can also protect your art. This is a bit of a moving target, but one you'll have to grasp as you move forward. I want to start by going back to something we discussed chapters ago: copyright law. As I've mentioned, music is protected by this law. BUT, if you were to invent an instrument—or a new part of an instrument—you'd have to get that protected via patent law.

But one more thing about copyright; it's important to do this for your own music. You can officially register, through the US copyright office, your musical work or sound recordings so that you're protected.

LET'S TALK ABOUT LAWYERS

For most of my career, until I was in my thirties, I had never had a need for lawyers. This was because, until then, most of my deals were cash and carry, or I dealt mainly with people who had companies that protected them, and, by extension, me. However, when I formed a business entity, in which I merged with a large corporate entity, I had to work with a lawyer on many levels. This taught me a great deal about not only the law, but how we—as artists and businesspeople—need to legally protect ourselves.

Basically, attorneys are necessary for many aspects of your professional career. They are an investment: attorneys are expensive, and they calculate their time carefully, and they don't like to waste it, especially if they know you don't have a lot of money. Don't present yourself as a major company, because they will charge you that way, and, quite frankly, what you may need help with may not require that level of attention or support. Be honest about your financial situation. Attorneys are human, after all! If they like what you do, they will work with you.

I find it's very helpful to start legal correspondence while knowing exactly what it is you need from a lawyer. But even before that, figure out how the fulfillment of your request can be accomplished with minimal correspondence.

Note that unless you get into a battle with someone, or a company, the level of legal protection you establish for your business will give you the ability to not have to worry about you, your assets, or your art. This next section will go more into depth in the area of attorneys.

WHEN DO YOU NEED A LAWYER?

When I was teaching my music business course at Edward Waters College early last spring, I invited my friend and attorney, Obi Ummuna, to visit to my class. During that day, I had my class create a project that they would have to design a budget for, and within these projects they listed every possible line item to make their event or business happen. Obi listened, and when he stood up to speak, he applauded them on the level of detail that was in their business plans. Then he asked my students, "Why are there no legal fees within your plans?"

He told my class something that I'm sharing with you today: if we don't involve lawyers, so much of what we create will not be sustained because it's simply not protected.

I have two wonderful attorneys whom I call on occasionally. The first one assisted me in setting up my business, Unanimous Music, as part of my company, Ulysses Owens Jr., LLC, and was the lawyer whom I used within a major business deal I spoke about earlier. My attorney gave me great advice, and because of him, I was able to have a strong and solid structure set up for future business endeavors that are separate from my career as a musician and educator.

The second attorney works primarily for my nonprofit organization and has been instrumental in assisting us with trademarking our brand. Setting up a nonprofit requires a particular legal skill set, and so I wanted to have expertise and advice in that area, and this what I am recommending to you, from someone who works in that domain. After all, nonprofits and for-profits are two totally different animals.

Lawyers are necessary; just discover the right one for your business endeavors, and don't be afraid to search for a while until you find the right fit. As far as finding the right one, word of mouth is a great way to find an attorney.

Let's talk about when you'll need a legal lens, or the support of an attorney.

CONTRACT REVIEW

Contracts will be, if they aren't already, a big part of your working life. As a creative artist, the minute you start recording albums with small or major labels, they are going to ask you to sign a contract. If you are going to be part of an Off-Broadway Show, or musical, they will ask for a contract. Even church jobs may request that you sign a letter of agreement, because the bigger the production and money involved, the more there needs to be a guarantee on your time. Also, if someone is part of a legitimate business, or company, there should be a contract involved at some point of the process. Some people may offer agreements in lieu of a contract; the objective is generally the same. Like a contract, in the case of an agreement, you may just include basic terms of the performance or opportunity, but not all of the extra contractual language.

Though some musicians I know really don't like contracts, they should be mutually beneficial agreements. After all, the goal in most cases is that they protect both parties. However, it's extremely important that any party who's about to sign a contract reads it and understands it. How can a lawyer help in this case? It's hugely helpful to have someone review a contract to make sure the terms are clear, and that they're in your best interest. A lawyer will also notice all the potential loopholes that are out there. Some lawyers will offer a flat fee for a contract review.

Do keep in mind that it's important to know what it takes to have an appropriate legal document to protect your work. When I first started drafting agreements, I thought it was merely enough to simply document what was spoken about in conversation with a client, but there are certain legal phrases and sentences that need to be handled properly to be protected in business.

CONTRACT LANGUAGE

Most lawyers will have several types of contract models, and most importantly, they will have contractual language for each one. This, to me, is honestly where lawyers get their worth. Anyone can write on a piece of paper some terms, date, and times, and the job that needs to be done. However, most lawyers know exactly how to write the various clauses that protect either you, or the company of inter-est that you are doing business with. Every word could be important on these documents, and often they are far from easy to understand. Consequently, many artists have been taken advantage of because they didn't get the language.

Again, I emphasize: it's important to get a lawyer to assist you, especially if you are working for a company that has a pre-existing contract model that is mostly in their favor. You want someone who speaks legalese who can help you decipher the language and objective of these contracts.

DRAFTING YOUR OWN CONTRACTS

Now, I've mentioned the cost of lawyers, and the fact that this can really be an expensive endeavor. So, if you're just starting out and can't find a lawyer who's devoted to your cause, what can you do?

Or what if you're working on a smaller-scale project, and just want a model that you can adjust and use—without paying high fees? Obi Ummuna, Esq., gave me some information for those who can't afford a lawyer. This info, which I'll share in a moment, has been helpful for me, and I have used it often.

SEVEN THINGS YOU NEED TO INCLUDE IN YOUR CONTRACT

These seven points are what Obi says are must-have elements in any contract you draft—or sign:

Pricing/rates

Do you get paid by the hour or flat fee or per service? What is the deposit policy? Quick aside: I think you should always take a deposit before you work. Clients always ask how much to take and there is no set answer. I usually tell people to never take less than 30%. If you have to buy supplies, your deposit should try to at least cover those.

Deliverables

What are you going to provide the client—and by when? This should be a clear list of tangible/measurable outcomes of everything that's going to be included. This can be set up as a kind of timeline, with milestones, and must have a final deadline as to when you expect to deliver the project. It also should include the delivery method (PDF, etc.).

Project scope

What are the expectations of the project? This is where you need to list what is required to achieve the goal of the project.

Payment/invoicing

How soon after completion will you get paid? Will it be a cash (or cash service) or check payment? Where will the check be sent? Another payment extra: I don't recommend the 50% up front and the 50% at the end payment system. I have seen a lot of people get stuck for the other 50%. I would recommend making payments correspond with deliverables along the way.

Single Point of Contact

Who has the final say? Who is the person who will be available to receive communications and coordinate responses to questions and concerns on behalf of the respective parties?

Early Termination

How do you end early? Sometimes things do not work out, and you need to end the project early. What happens and how much do you get paid?

Revisions, Rewrites, Changes

During the course of the project, the client may change his or her mind. What happens then? Does it change the price? How?

STARTING BUSINESSES

Lawyers are also instrumental in helping you with the infrastructure of a business, as well as registering your corporation. As you work through the creation of a business plan, choose a name, a team, and identify your sources of funding, it's helpful to speak with an attorney who can not only advise you how to set it up as far as structure, but also help you legally protect and solidify the business.

There are various business structures that your lawyer can help you set up:

- LLC
- Sole Proprietorship
- S Corp
- Enterprise
- Partnerships
- Not for Profit
- For Profit

Again, a lawyer will be able to guide you through the benefits of each of the setups. Additionally, as there are with all businesses, state, and city laws, and codes will have to be considered as well. Again, the right attorney will help you with navigating all of this successfully.

TRADEMARKING

With businesses, logos, names, and ideas, you will want to trademark them, because many times you can build a successful brand and someone who is not as creative will come and trademark your idea and make money off of it.

To this point, I watched a Netflix documentary about Robert John Burck, also known as the Naked Cowboy, in New York City. Being from New York, I distinctly remember when this guy started showing up in Times Square with, literally, just his underwear (briefs), cowboy boots, a cowboy hat, and a guitar. He would sometimes sing songs, but mostly he would just take pictures with people. Apparently, someone was smart enough to advise him to trademark his name and his image. Today he is very rich, not only because he capitalized on his image then, but because he actually is still capitalizing on it.

MANAGERS CAN ALSO PROTECT YOU

A good friend and colleague said, "You need a manager when you can no longer manage your life and career." Lawyers are huge protectors of your art, but there are other, additional sources of guidance and protection. As stated in this quote, they can help facilitate and guide your life as a musical professional. Many musicians express their desire to have a manager to sort out all kinds of professionally relevant aspects of their lives. I remind them, as I remind you, that of course hiring a manager—as in the case of hiring the previous protectors—can be pricey. This is not an investment to be taken lightly. But it is a good investment and, when you do start working more, you'll need one. Here, I'm offering some tips in regard to finding the right manager for you.

Look for the following:

Successful track records

You should be able to look at the management company or manager and see the level of success they've helped others achieve. Be careful to not compare, or expect them to do the same thing for your career. Nevertheless, it's important to know they can make something happen. You also want them to be independently successful; they should be able to stand on their own reputation, not just yours.

Someone who walks through the door with a plan, not an invoice

Many managers approached me early on in my career, just when I began to make some traction and have steady work. A lot of them wanted commission on that work—the work that I had secured on my own. This was my clear indication that they were not the right fits for me.

I find that we have to really test people's motivation for working with us. When a manager wants to get commission on relationships you have already built before them, I would question whether they're going to be effective. After all, it's their job to bring new relationships and partnerships on board in order to create economic gains that will benefit everyone. You also want someone who is not too busy juggling other clients. A manager needs to devote the personalized attention that you need.

Someone who's realistic

Okay—I've spoken about being real before, but it's important. In my case, I definitely love when people speak highly of me; I think all of us do, because we all have egos that like to be fed! However, I like managers when they are realistic with me about my goals, as well as sincere estimates as to how long it will take for certain goals will come to fruition. My management team now has been very helpful and realistic with my career desires and what's actually possible, and I respect them greatly for that.

Someone who's got juice

I like managers who have connections and influence that I don't have and who can bring that to my career. If I walk into the room with a manager and no one knows him or her, it raises caution for me. I clearly recognize that my goal is to be known and navigate the scene successfully. If my manager is an unknown, how can I hire him or her to represent me? Also, you should make sure that manager is known specifically in the circle you want to have influence in. If that person is masterful and connected in the Broadway world, but you want to be a jazz star, maybe it's cause for concern.

Someone who's a connector

Ultimately, your manager needs to connect—to take your career, your plans, and their own vision of your career and connect you to others who can make that possible, while simultaneously protecting you as an entity and investment.

Your manager should also be working with a booking agent. The booking agent, is—on a different level—another protector; the agent is the one that gets work for you. This person works with your manager, and potentially the record company. They make sure that work is coming to you. Both you and your manager will work closely with a booking agent to help them understand which of your projects or bands will be appropriate for certain venues/certain levels of success. A booking agent can also protect you as a product on the road and stand in between you and venue to facilitate the issuing of the right contracts that will protect you.

If your manager doesn't have an effective strategy for your career, nor the resources to execute it, then you are working with the wrong person.

Reflections for thought and discussion:

1. Have you ever had to protect—or wanted to protect—any of your creations?
2. Why did you or didn't you do it?

3. Have you ever signed an agreement or contract related to your work as an artist?
4. Explain the situation.
5. Have you ever drafted a contract or an agreement?
6. Do you have a lawyer you can use at this phase of your career?

Reflections for writing:

1. Research some of the businesses listed in this chapter (like LLC, S Corp, Enterprise, etc.). Write down the top three that appeal to you most—and why.
2. If you were meeting a potential manager, what would be the top five questions you'd ask in an interview? Write them down.
3. Write down your primary three expectations for a manager.
4. Write down your primary three expectations for a booking agent regarding booking desires and territories you want your project to tour in.

CHAPTER 14
Financial Management and Funding an Idea

"My parents always taught me that my job would never make me rich; it'd be my homework."—Daymond John, American Businessman, Investor, Television Personality, Author and Motivational Speaker

Financial management comes hand-in-hand with relevant knowledge, and can be achieved through various realizations, as well as assistance from different people. Independent knowledge is key as far as setting career financial goals; I classify this knowledge as a kind of awareness, which includes budgeting and goal setting, paired with a realization about oneself and what one needs to survive initially, and then to enjoy. Moving beyond that basic stage comes the next phase: funding an idea. This chapter includes financial management tails and tips on how to attain necessary—and appropriate—funds.

MY TALE

Years ago, I was a full-time member of the Kurt Elling Quartet. I joined back in August 2010, and pretty much from the moment I joined Kurt's band, we took off on a plane to Tel Aviv, Israel, and returned home a week later. Then we went on a two-week tour of the west coast of the USA. After that, we went to Europe for all of

November. When we got home from that very successful tour, Kurt's manager, the great Mary Ann Topper, called us and declared, "Guys, pack your bags! You are going to Russia."

Then we got home from Russia, were lucky to enjoy the holidays with the family, and she summoned us once again. Even before the New Year could get started, she said France was calling. We toured France for over two weeks.

We kept that pace for about two years straight. Touring that much took me from struggling financially to being able to do more than pay my bills. I was now able to build a lifestyle because I had consistent financial support.

During that same time, I received a call from Christian McBride's manager, and he asked me to substitute some dates for Christian's drummer at the time, and I toured the west coast with him for a week and half, and I thought that was it. Well, after I unpacked my bags and started to settle back in at home, his manager called again, and asked me to go Europe to tour with Christian for a few more weeks. When I returned from Europe, I began to tour with Kurt and Christian simultaneously, and then also with Nicholas Payton.

I went from not having a job to being able to tour with three bands at the same time. This completely shifted my financial status, and I got used to the steady work. I even started making certain financial decisions based on this new surge of income from three different sources. Until one really important day.

THE END OF AN ERA

And then it happened: Kurt Elling got called to do an all-star tour, which was amazing for him and his career, but it put his band—which included me at that point—on a hiatus with very limited work. Still, I was okay, because I had just started touring more with McBride. However, the following year, McBride got called to do the same tour, and that put us on a hiatus as well.

And that, dear students, was when I went through one of the most difficult financial periods of my life.

I realized after that moment that I needed to nurture multiple relationships and establish multiple streams of income so that I was no longer financially held hostage by the decisions other bandleaders needed to make for their careers. It's not their job to keep me working, or to make my life financially stable. It's an honor to work with them, but I have to take care of myself and work on multiple opportunities so that I am never in need.

PLANNING AHEAD

I learned now that, when touring or recording or however you are making more money, or your income is at an all-time high, it's important to save. Believe me, at some point, things will slow down and potentially become uncomfortably tight. Because of this, I advise all of you to save, and to learn how to save aggressively. The life of a freelance artist can be quite financially unstable at times. You may go through moments where you are making a lot of money, and then moments that are average.

If you can plan ahead and save so that you can cover the minimum during those slow moments, it will allow you to be taken care of and enjoy the rest that comes with not having a jam-packed schedule.

When that—a total slow down—first happened to me, I was unprepared both financially and emotionally. In fact, going through that experience several times is what personally made me fall out of love with being a sideman, and pushed me to get myself into a position where I control more of my destiny and am no longer dependent upon someone else's work flow to determine my financial flow.

FINANCIAL ARRANGEMENTS FOR PRODUCERS

When I first started producing records, it wasn't for money: I just wanted to be knowledgeable about the process, make great records, and please the client. Being a producer had been something I wanted so bad, and a lot of my initial clients didn't really know if they needed a producer and they certainly didn't know if I was going to be the best person for their record, so I really put in a lot of time and sweat equity and took very small fees. Actually, the first record that I produced, I did for free, and I told the artist that if they didn't like the record, they at least didn't have to pay me for it. They liked it, thankfully—and so did I.

My first financial arrangement with producing records was to set a fee, whereby I would receive a deposit of 50% when we started rehearsals and recordings. When the mastered CD was completed, I then requested the rest of the payment. I wanted the artist to know that my focus was truly their creative happiness.

The problem with that payment arrangement that I listed earlier is that it didn't always for work. For example, many times artists would get nervous during the process, or they would just be in shock and have to get comfortable with the sound of their own voices.

In conclusion, make sure an artist is comfortable with who they are before you produce and record with them; otherwise, during this process, every insecurity imaginable will arise because the microphone tells no lies. At that point, they will blame you, the producer, for their own inadequacies musically, so don't get caught in that fight. Additionally, make sure you are adequately compensated, no matter what happens. After that experience, I had to build in multiple clauses that allowed me to be compensated for the hours, days, and months of work separate from someone's dissatisfaction with their own musical skills.

FINANCIAL TIPS TO START

I remember when I first got signed by my booking agent, and my group had a huge tour booked, and I was so excited about it—my dreams were coming true. Then, someone from my management team called me about four months before the tour and they said, "Ulysses, we are ready to book the plane tickets for the tour, because they are at a reasonable price now and it will allow you to make more money if we book them now."

I was in. I thought the deposit from the venue was going to go towards my plane tickets. Unfortunately, that was not the case—nor is it the usual process. Instead, I had to figure out how I was going to front several thousand dollars months in advance while waiting on the reimbursements. That's when I realized that having access to cash is not only helpful, but also necessary. Also, having good credit is huge, because you will need to purchase tickets with a credit card and maintain that until you play the gigs, and subsequently reimburse yourself. This was a real wakeup call, and honestly, when I became a bandleader, I had to become more financially savvy, because as a bandleader I was responsible for others as well.

USING CREDIT CARDS

I wish someone would have taught me, especially while in college, that I needed to be careful about credit card debt. In my family, we didn't really talk about that, but when I all of sudden needed to finance plane tickets, I thankfully had a decent credit rating, so I was able to secure a credit card that had a decent limit, and allowed me to handle my business.

Let's talk a bit more about credit—and credit cards. Credit cards are necessary when you are a bandleader, period. As a bandleader, you will have to spend a lot of money buying plane tickets and fronting money for tours, etc. One tour could put you in a position of fronting $10K–$15K, and then getting your money back when the tour is complete.

Even as a sideman, you should have a credit card. Despite the fact that you can perhaps operate without a card if you travel domestically, once you start traveling extensively domestically and internationally, it's important to have one. Even for simple things like incidentals at a hotel or a car rental, a credit card is useful tool.

But a credit card can be financially dangerous if you're not careful. Paying your bills on time and maintaining the right credit balances and limits are really important. I am not a financial advisor, but I list these subjects in the book because as a creative, you need to be aware of the financial ramifications of all aspects of your work.

And so, dear students, don't "forget" about that bill; credit card fees can be astronomical, and while it might feel good to have that money once you do get paid, I urge you to put it right back into covering those bills as needed. As I mentioned, I did not understand this in college, and had to make sure that I cleared away a lot of the unnecessary debt and mistakes I accumulated in college to make room to have the necessary amount of credit for my businesses.

CREDIT SCORE

I want to briefly talk about credit rating. Basically, every individual has an opportunity to build credit attached to your social security number. Oddly enough, having no credit is sometimes worse than having bad credit. A credit score affects your ability to garner credit cards, loans, a house, car, and business loans. It's important to manage your credit score by paying your bills on time, and making sure they are not late. If, for some reason, you pay your bills late and they get turned over to the collections department, it's important to satisfy and settle those debts as quickly as you possibly can. All of these are realities that can either help you reach your goals, or, conversely, prohibit them artistically.

HIRE AN ACCOUNTANT

One of the ways that you can help yourself manage finances is by getting outside help. With legal issues, you go—as I suggested in the last chapter—to an attorney. In the case of finances, you should go to an accountant.

It's important to work with a CPA (certified public accountant), someone who is certified, because money is a real issue for artists. Having someone who is certified and skilled on how to help you handle your finances will save you a lifetime of money problems and emotional and mental headaches.

There are some musicians I have met who are smart enough to coordinate all of their finances AND manage to do their own taxes. I am not one of them. Especially because most of us are technically freelance artists, learning how to manage money and cash flow is a huge part of sustaining a career and a lifestyle, as is learning to, at times, adjust the lifestyle for the moments when things will shift financially.

Vet your accountant, and make sure they know how to work with musicians and creatives. We have a different set of rules that apply to our finances. The more you document and have clear records of your tax information and financial information, the easier you will make it for your accountants.

TAXES

Let's talk a bit more about taxes. First, I'll share my experience; when I started making over $40K of non-taxed income, I all of a sudden started having major problems with taxes. I began to get these large tax bills, and finally, I met an accountant who urged me to start my LLC. This was one of the greatest things that I could have done, because any income that your LLC makes is not taxed. You only get taxed on what your LLC pays you. Also, I was able to write off all of the various expenses that it requires to be a creative.

For those who start to work with vendors, promoters, and companies, who are paying other musicians and people, you really need to get with an experienced accountant who understands how to work with creatives. I stopped going to H&R Block in college because once your income starts flowing differently, it's important to hire someone who knows how to work with you. Otherwise, it will cost you a lot of money and potential problems with the IRS.

And you don't want problems with the IRS!

WHAT IS A TAX DEDUCTION?

A good accountant will help you navigate the arena of tax deductions. For example, when you purchase something like a piece of musical gear for $100.00, you then get to take the amount and deduct it from your income tax, because what you purchased was necessary to your career. Instead of taxing that $100.00, you can count it as a loss, and Uncle Sam won't be waiting in line to tax that money.

However, as an individual, there is a limit to how much money you can deduct. As an artist in NYC, for example, they only allow you up to a certain point of deductions from your income. This will be very important for you to ascertain depending on where you live.

Thankfully, in my case, that first accountant who helped me start my LLC was tremendously helpful. This—setting up the LLC—allowed me to start receiving payments to my LLC, and then paying myself a salary from that LLC. Thanks to this, I only have to pay taxes from what I pay myself personally. What this means is that once I became an LLC, my tax bills decreased majorly to something that I could actually manage.

Today, I am really thankful to have the current accounting team that I work with, because they taught me to document everything regarding my finances so that I could avoid one of the most painful things to experience: being at the mercy of the IRS.

Oh yes, the IRS. The IRS is not your friend. So, dear students, one of the fundamental purposes of this book was for me to provide information for you and so that you could learn from my mistakes. I have a relevant tale to tell:

I had a situation years ago where my previous accountant had not reminded me of payroll taxes that I owed for my LLC. With that said, I was behaving normally, not realizing that I owed the IRS funds, and not realizing that they had every intention to collect. So, I was out to dinner, and the last stop before I got home with my girlfriend at the time was a cigar bar. We had a nice cigar and a drink, and when the bill came, the waitress politely asked for my card and I gave it to her. It's important for you to know that I am very anal about my finances and always have a ballpark figure in my mind of what I have in my bank account.

The waitress came back and quietly announced that my card had been declined. Of course, I was embarrassed, but also perplexed, because I knew I had more than enough money in my account to handle the charge.

I pulled up my account information on my phone. I looked at my balance, which was fine, but it was in red, and next to it, it read, "Please contact the IRS."

My stomach fell to the bottom of the floor. Long story short, my girlfriend took care of the bill. (I paid her back, of course.)

That night, I called the bank, who announced that they were powerless: "Mr. Owens, there is nothing we can do; you have to settle this with the IRS."

The next day, I settled it, paid the debt, and they un-froze my account. I had no idea how powerful the IRS was, but I now understand that they have the ability to make your life very difficult if you don't pay your taxes.

In conclusion, dear students, it's important to heed my words of advice: you have to pay your taxes. Hire a great accountant who can advise you on whether to pay quarterly or, even if you get an outstanding tax debt, on how to set up to pay installment agreements.

COMPENSATION

I have had many challenges through the years, but one of the first things I needed to do was to not be afraid of money, and also to not be afraid to ask questions to other professional jazz musicians about money. I also needed advice on how to successfully navigate the financial aspects of our world.

I remember years ago, when I first started working professionally in Jacksonville, Florida, I would work with some employers who weren't up-front about the amount of money I was going to be paid, and even worse, wouldn't tell me when I was going to be paid. So my mother told me, "Stop coming home without clarity, because your father and I can't do anything about it. Find out directly from the bandleader when and what they are going to pay you, and be nice about it."

This taught me to really be to learn to be clear with people and, in a kind way, to ask them what their intentions were pertaining to money. This—removing the layer of that concern simply by communicating—was great advice, and helped me move forward in that arena.

In general, I don't like to argue about money. Obviously, over the years, as I gained more experience, I expected to be compensated more appropriately for my time. I try to work with people to reach that agreement professionally. I always tell people, "I play for free, but my time is what costs, and it can be expensive."

As I now have more things competing for my time, I have started to require a higher minimum to guarantee my time, especially far in advance. However, I think it's really important to make sure that you work with the artist and employer according to their budget. Living in New York City teaches you to be very realistic about the amount of money you can charge, because there is always someone who will work for cheaper. The goal, I feel, is to get the experience first, and then navigate the money. Still, I never forget the reality that I love music and I want to always be making music.

No one can tell you how much money you need to be making, but you can definitely have a number in mind and work with that employer to get as close to that number as possible. Keep in mind, however, that especially in this industry, work begets work, so the more you are working, the better it will look to those who are considering you for other opportunities. I always say that with compensation, you should be flexible, yet realistic with what the market is suggesting for the amount of work you are going to do.

DOCUMENT YOUR COMPENSATION

Years ago, I started keeping a little steno pad with my pay for gigs, and it's helped me to keep track of what I am getting paid and know how to really grow towards my earning goals and be aware of what I have been paid in the past. Right now, I love using the Apple Notes feature to create my monthly financial plans, and I can easily transfer them to an Excel document if I need to. I also have my business bank and credit card statements go directly to my accountant so they can manage my "P&L Documents" (profit and loss), which is essential to monthly bookkeeping for LLCs.

Also, if and when you seek to buy a car or home or rent an apartment, you are going to need to know what income you have access to, especially if you have the kind of career where you are being paid cash constantly. Keep records of your income, because it will be necessary as you seek to build a lifestyle.

INVOICING

If you seek to be a musician and creative who not only plays creative gigs, but also works with additional vendors and other companies, you will need to have an invoicing system to be able to do business professionally. I am a stickler for invoices and how they are presented. I don't approve someone just asking me to pay them; compensation must be requested by an invoice. Also, as an artist, I have had other musicians request invoices from me.

It's important to get a sample of some acceptable templates that can work for invoicing. I use www.WaveApps.com, and though they charge a small fee, it works well. You can input your gig information, and they can even accept electronic and credit card payments from the payee. Presentation is very important regarding invoices, so take the time to create a professional invoice, which includes having the information not only accurately presented, but also correctly spelled. Make sure you always double-check—and then check again—before submitting.

FINANCIALLY SURVIVING LIFE ON THE ROAD

This was probably one of the biggest adjustments financially that I had to endure for many years. It's one thing to be an artist in your home-town or in a city where you have friends who can assist you through your challenges. It's another thing when you are across the sea in foreign lands and dealing with challenges of surviving on the road. The goal is to make sure that you are smart—and secure—during your travels.

While some tours will provide per-diem for you, others simply will not. Also, as far as your hotel room, make sure you have them clarify about incidentals, and that they aren't charging you for the room and tax.

Either way, you will need a credit card from Visa or MasterCard, because not every country will willingly accept American Express because it's a higher vendor charge. This will be helpful with hotels needing a card for incidentals. Also, be sure that you notify your bank prior to traveling so that they don't cut off your credit when you're abroad.

Here are some money—and comfort-relevant—tips for you:

- Find a grocery store: This will make it cheaper to not have to eat out every night.
- Locate a pharmacy: This is for first-aid and other relevant needs.
- Choose the right kind of ATM: Make sure you go to one— if possible—inside a bank. When you choose random ATMs, you can open yourself up to fraudulent attacks.

As far as comfort, be sure to travel with vitamins and any medicine that you need. Also, bring things that make you happy—incense, candles, etc.

A singer friend of mine came on the road with me once, and I happened to stop by her room to borrow something. When I walked in, I saw that she had turned the room into this beautiful zen space. She had brought her own fabrics and beautifully draped them to create a space that was similar to her home. Actually, I do the same: I bring my speakers, books, and whatever is going to keep me in the right space and focused.

Some musicians with dietary issues travel with their own blenders and groceries to make their food. Again, bring what makes you comfortable and happy. The key, I feel, is to look at the life you lead at your home and figure out how much of that can you take with you when you travel.

Getting back to the theme of this chapter, it's also important that you're smart BEFORE you get on the road financially and make sure all of your bills are paid. Or you can access them online, so you don't return from the road to put out financial fires.

CAREER FINANCIAL GOALS

We've gone through several financial scenarios as far how you can set yourself up and protect yourself.

As an artist you go through a few different financial stages once you start making money:

1. You are excited to be able to make money and eat and invest back into your career.
2. You are excited to make money that can provide stability for yourself—like food, shelter, and basic needs.
3. You have surpassed the level of having basic needs being covered, and now you can save and live more of a lifestyle, and may have even found others to invest in what you want to accomplish in your career.
4. You have now been placed in a situation where now you are thinking about your future and potentially those who are going to be part of your future with the money you are starting to make.

Ultimately in this career, you want to make sure that you set financial goals for yourself and work towards their attainment.

I've been careful about my steps: in my life and career, I always set certain goals and then find jobs that would provide the means by which I could attain them. I recognized from early on that I had chosen a life that would cause my finances to go through some changes or be in a state of flux. This is because as an artist, as much money as you make, you have to invest back in your career. You are your own bank and investor for many years.

I want you to also have this self-awareness and foresight. I want to challenge all of you to set financial goals for yourself and seek to accomplish them.

I always said I am a jazz musician, but I refuse to live like the stereotypical jazz musician: broke, destitute, living from pillar to post, but a creative genius. Actually, that is not my idea of genius at all.

What is smart in my book—among other things—is having the foresight to plan ahead for both financial security and protection.

Budgeting

This is especially a challenge when you have a financial flow that is not always consistent, but you should know the amount of money you need to cover your expenses. Consider what you need as a bare minimum, and then what would be great to earn.

LIFESTYLE FINANCIAL DECISIONS

As I mentioned, my goal is to have you pay attention to certain fundamentals regarding your finances. Believe me, I didn't always know this, and am forever grateful to people who guided me—as I've also mentioned.

A few years ago, I was playing a gig at Jazz at Lincoln Center a few years ago, and I met a lovely woman, a fan for years, who was a financial advisor. She generously offered to enlighten me about her field, and I subsequently realized that there was very little that I had established for myself in the way of protection of my financial assets.

As a financial advisor, she was well versed in different products that are designed to help people in various stages of their earnings. This can protect you now, as your financial scenarios change, and of course as you get older. Because we artists may not have many of the corporate benefits that those who work in different situations might have, we need to educate ourselves, and protect ourselves accordingly. Here are some points for consideration and discussion, once your finances increase:

- Owning a home
- IRA
- 401(k)
- Stocks and bonds
- CDs
- Investments

Of course, there's more to this field, but this is what I want to put on your radar. But I'm going to add to this list:

- Life insurance
- Will and testament

Now stay with me! I know many of you are young and might balk at this. But these products are equally important. Honestly, I'm a bit tired of seeing so many musicians who are gifted and who have touched the world with their gift, and then they leave their families so ill-equipped financially when they die. I have seen so many GoFundMe and other crowdfunding initiatives to help musicians just merely get by, and I think it's because we aren't having that conversation now.

So, to the millennials and centennials, let's not have this issue. With each new generation should come another level of knowledge and wisdom, allowing us to navigate the world more successfully.

Please purchase life insurance, which will take care of your funeral expenses, and also leave your family with some financial support in your absence. Also, make sure you file a will and testament to designate your legacy, and how what you leave behind gets distributed to the world.

Many of us have album masters, projects, art, and a continual list of things that will be a great asset to a library, or communities, and we must articulate that on a will and testament.

I had dinner with some colleagues from the Erroll Garner Foundation, which is a great foundation that preserves the work and legacy of the pianist Erroll Garner. It was amazing to me how Erroll's manager and wife, Martha Glaser, really took care of him while he was living, but even more so after his death. She spent twenty to thirty years after his life cataloguing all of his music, and now there is an entire foundation that has been releasing albums and educating people about his legacy. Most creatives will leave a rich and profound legacy, and it's going to be pivotal for us to have the right people in our lives to help us make those decisions now.

LIVING BENEATH YOUR MEANS

Learn to live beneath your means to accomplish major stuff. Some of my closest friends who are incredibly successful in the business have learned how to really live an economically minimal life so that they could finance their artistic lives.

SUPPLEMENTAL CAREERS

You may have to find a supplemental job, or make a career move that can allow you to bring your creative plans and ideas to fruition.

FINANCIAL ADVICE FOR FUNDING AN IDEA

Many times, we have ideas for shows, CDs, books, and anything else you can imagine, but we lack the funds to make that happen. In those cases, we need to go beyond to look for monies to help make our dreams a reality. How do we ask for money for our dreams? As one colleague says, "Look people in the eye, engage them, and make them feel like they are investing in something they desire as much as you." This is great advice for anything we're trying to sell: we need to take that idea and present it with the passion we feel about it.

What's important to acknowledge is that there are people out in the world who sincerely want to bring artistic dreams to fruition because people need art and experiences. There are many different ways to secure funds. In this section, I will go through several.

But first, how do you know if your ideas is a good one?

Just because you thought about it or created it doesn't necessarily qualify it to be funded. So, how can this happen? You need to figure out how to structure your creative idea and see if it's even fundable.

Here's a kind of checklist you can run your ideas through:

- Is this idea just about you?
- Is this idea just a creative riff?
- Is this creative idea going to solve a problem?

- How large is the idea?
- Can this idea be executed on a small scale?
- Who is benefiting from this idea?
- Who needs this idea? Do they need it now?
- Can you fund this idea on your own?
- If you had the money, would you fund this idea?

Once you go through this list, you need to answer this question after removing any emotional attachment: Is this idea worthy of funding? If the answer is yes, then, by all means, keep it moving forward!

PRESENTING AN IDEA VS. BEGGING

To be honest, during most of my career, I have never gotten a lot of financial assistance. I have had to leverage my own finances and credit to make stuff happen. However, there is one person who is incredibly generous, and I am not going to list his name, just to protect his identity. He and his family are above and beyond gracious to many musicians and artists. I asked him once what he looks for when considering giving to an artist. He answered, "There are two things I look for: seriousness and ability to work hard, and talent."

With that said, if you are seeking funding, the question is, what have you done up to that point? I can definitely say that I have exhausted myself in working and figuring out plans to make things work, and only when I absolutely had nowhere else to turn would I reach out to someone for help.

HOW TO RAISE MONEY

This is the million-dollar question—literally. I was speaking with a key fundraising person at a major institution, and she gave me some great advice about raising money for various projects. One of the key things she explained was that you first need to make sure that people know that they matter to you. No one wants to feel like all they are worth to you is a checkbook.

In my case, I have started giving money to various friends who are raising money, and I always give first to:

- People who have a great idea.
- People who are seeking to create an idea or project that shows a selfless side of them.
- People who are impacting a community that needs it.

These are the criteria I look for because I want to contribute to causes I agree with so that I can support both them and their mission.

FUNDING FOR A NONPROFIT

When my family and I started our nonprofit, Don't Miss a Beat (DMAB), my mother became director of development. She handles fundraising, and she is really good at it. We have seen consistent and exponential growth from the beginning of our existence. However, a few years ago, there were certain projects and ideas that I had related to the efforts of our nonprofit. She suggested, "Ulysses, why don't you approach certain people for the funding, because they believe not only in the nonprofit, but also in your personal efforts. They've always asked me to come to them if there were an additional idea that needed help."

I was really nervous about doing this, but instead of approaching it like I needed something, I took a different route. In the end, these are people who, even if they never gave me anything, I would enjoy being around them. So, I just looked at the moments we shared as a chance to hang out with cool people. When I was more relaxed and at ease, I was able to articulate certain funding needs—without directly requesting, and without begging. This was a way I felt comfortable with, and apparently, they did, too.

I am not an expert at raising money, and there are definitely tons of other books you should and can read about that. What I will do is give advice as a creative on how to leverage your talent and what you are already great at to gain people's interest. Here are my tips:

Forget about the money; put money out of your mind and focus on connecting with people

When we are on stage as performers, we aren't worried about how much money we are making at that moment. We are merely trying to connect our craft to the audience to get them to feel the joy we feel from making art. That's how I feel about raising money—let's just connect people to the joy of what we do, and figure out what matters to them, and get them interested in us and our journey. If you have someone's interest, then support (money) will follow.

Be genuine

People with limitless amounts of money and resources can smell a "taker" a mile away, and chances are they are constantly trying to get far away from those who only value them for their money. I urge you to be honest—genuine—in your mission and, if it ties into their interests as well, those who see value in you and your ideas will support you financially.

Think long-term

Even as someone who is generous, I try not to give to people who I know won't care about me at all once I write the check. Make the connection, and it may take months or even years for that person to support you, but once they start, they won't stop. I have donors now who didn't start giving until maybe five or six years into our business because they watched us and wanted to see if this was a short-term business or something that would last and grow. Now that we are in our eleventh year, they are on board and bring other people to the table.

Be consistent in communication

You have to be consistent in communication with people, and I find that so many creatives FAIL at this task. Their minds are so up in the clouds regarding themselves, and they become so self-absorbed and yet can't fund their own projects. Communication builds a community.

BUILDING A DONOR BASE

You can apply much of what I wrote about earlier to building a donor base, but there are a few other components.

First, you need to consider, who is your donor base?

First-time donors

You have to research and figure out who the signature and unique donors are who are going to start their giving journey with you. Many people who started giving to DMAB had never given to an organization like that. So, it's great to get those people interested in you and your mission.

Within Jacksonville, Florida, there is an arts community and a large amount of people who love supporting the arts. After a few years of existence, we began to tap into that community of supporters who love the arts, and, by virtue of the fact that our organization is arts-focused, some of those donors became interested in the work that we do, and started giving.

Corporate donors

This is a big bear, and you will need to involve a grant-writer to really tackle the bigger corporations. They have large and complex bureaucratic systems set up around their giving and how they distribute donations.

In-kind donations

This was the way that we sustained DMAB, in addition to our own constant giving to our business. In-kind donations can be someone giving their time, or donating products, or services, and we have amassed a lot of support this way. Many times, dollars aren't all that you need, especially if your business or organization will operate within a physical structure that requires daily upkeep. Garner in-kind support as well, because it will be very helpful to your mission.

Crowdfunding

I have mixed feelings about this as a resource, but I have to write about it, because it is a legitimate source of funding for many people and has been very helpful to them. What I will say is this: I have done one crowdfunding source years ago, for when my DMAB kids took a trip to Paris. At that time within the organization, our donor pool was small and resources were very limited, so we had to go outward to gain support, and, thankfully, we were successful.

Why do I have some negative impressions of crowdfunding? Sometimes I feel some people rely on others to make their dreams come true, and I don't think that's fair. Yet there are other artists who want to create more, so they tap into their fan base to gain support, which is great. You have to figure out what works for you.

Crowdfunding can be really impactful, and there are various channels: GoFundMe, Indie Gogo, Kickstarter, Patreon, and many others. As far as what they charge, percentages may vary, while others only compensate you if you reach your fundraising goal.

You will need to do some homework to find the platform that best works for you.

Competitions

I laughed the other day with one of my friends and said to him that I think we, as jazz musicians today, are living in the age of competitions. There are so many contests/competitive opportunities that potentially reward assistance to musicians with record deals, management, agency support, and other unique relationships. As a drummer, there aren't too many that apply to me, but I will say that if you are a pianist, composer, vocalist, or horn player, there are many resources. Some of these competitions can even allow you to gain money for anything related to your career and give you a great start.

Research online, and I am certain you will discover competitions and grants even that will assist with financial needs.

Fellowships

Fellowships are awarded opportunities that typically come from institutions where they will allow you to spend a concentrated amount of time on campus, or at the institution or organization, and it can even be a paid opportunity. Through these fellowships, you have a chance to study and gain further knowledge about your area of focus. Fellowships can be a great way to develop a work or idea that you may have wanted to focus on for a really long time, and the institution or organization that grants you the fellowship will work with you, support your efforts, and aid in your completing your idea successfully, or at least advancing it to the next stage.

Residencies

In some cases, a residency may be what you need if you are developing a larger work, and you need the time to develop the concept and figure out key components of what will make it work. Many foundations have housing paired with opportunities that can allow you to develop your work more fully.

Grants

Grants are often an ideal way to get funding for an idea, organization, or tour you desire to facilitate, and it's essentially free funding for you and your artistry. Grants are often highly competitive and usually require advanced planning as far as the application process.

Additionally, grant writing is a specialty; it's not something that can or should be taken lightly for several reasons. First, programs are very specific about the grantees they will fund. It's important to build both your platform and résumé to be able to be considered amongst the other potential grant awardees.

Grant writing

Grant writing is a special skill. For this reason, many organizations hire grant writers. Despite the fact that you may, in some cases, be able to get copies of sample submissions head of time, this is a specialty that you might not want to risk your talent on. They have to be written according to the focus of what the grant funders want to fund, not just the focus of needed money for your idea. If you are trying, and struggling with this task, I recommend engaging a professional grant writer.

Personally, I have had several grants that I did not receive initially, and I confess that was crushed. Consequently, I had to work extra hard to encourage myself to recover and use that rejection as an opportunity to ask the grant panel why I wasn't chosen. I didn't do this in an argumentative way, but in a way that would allow me to receive constructive criticism and relative guidance. I had hoped that by doing so, I would have the chance to re-tool my info, revamp my platform as needed, and then I might be suitable for the grant at a later time.

One of the grants I applied to was the very prestigious Chamber Music America (CMA) New Jazz Works grant, which I had heard about from various colleagues. I was very excited about applying for what promised to be a fabulous opportunity. When I received notice that I didn't get the grant, I requested a meeting to hear why. I was granted the privilege, and subsequently met two lovely and impressive people: Gargi and Susan.

Gargi sat down with me, and we didn't even speak about the grant; she asked me about what I was doing at that time, and what I was interested in. We begin to speak about this desire I had to lecture around the topic of music business and entrepreneurship. She told me that, given my platform as a musician, this was something rare, and that I should really pursue the idea. Shortly after, I was invited to present my workshop at the CMA "Next Gen" conference. And that, dear students, is how I started my journey of lecturing around the country, and now you are reading my book about it.

So, though I didn't receive the grant, I got something much greater: what that taught me was not to focus so much on the loss, but to figure out what direction I'm supposed to be running in. Many times, losing or not obtaining everything forces you to make other considerations.

Have a plan B

And that leads me to this next part about funding: the plan B.

A dear and very talented friend of mine was on the road and was approached by a wealthy person, who said he would like to invest in her career by creating the opportunity to take her career to the next level. My friend called me, and we went to work: we drafted a pretty detailed proposal of what she would love to accomplish and how much it would cost.

Once she presented the plan to the potential funder, she didn't hear from him again. This brings me to one of my key messages here: I have to be completely honest with you—most of your wildest dreams of attracting a donor or someone to financially pave the way for your career will not come to fruition. Or if it does, there may be some potential strings attached that you might not want to be connected to.

For this reason, I have spent most of my career making things happen on my own. When I have waited or hoped that people would chip in and help, it simply never happened. Most of the things I wanted to financially make happen required me to put some serious sweat in the game. I say this for all of you who may have potential donors: do not commit to anything until the funding has been approved and the check is in the bank.

That being said, there will definitely be some angel investors you will encounter in your life who are exceptionally kind. Make sure you appreciate those folks and thank them for their support.

Finding supporting angels is still quite rare, and sometimes as artists, it's an easy cop-out to hope for people to come in and save the day and support your project. If you won't invest in you, what makes you think you'll be able to motivate others to do the same on your behalf?

Most people mean well, though they don't always do well, so it's important to create a "Plan B," that is completely separate from needing the support of external resources to make your project happen. I have at times had to dig into my savings, or even, early in my career when I wasn't financially secure enough to even have a savings, spent money and figured out ways to earn it back by simply working hard.

Either way, the only one you can count on for sure is yourself and potentially close friends and family. This being said, on a certain level, what allows me to maintain great friendships is that I never ask my friends or family for money, because I firmly believe it's my responsibility to secure the necessary financial resources to make things happen in my career.

Reflections for thought and discussion:

1. Have you ever pursued funding for an idea? What happened?
2. What type of financial planning have you done?
3. What might you do now that you read this chapter?
4. What are some of your financial goals?

Reflections for writing:

1. Write down at least three ideas for which you might need to pursue funding.
2. Choose one and run it through the checklist:
   - Is this idea just about you?
   - Is this idea just a creative riff?
   - Is this creative idea going to solve a problem?
   - How large is the idea?
   - Can this idea be executed on a small scale?
   - Who is benefiting from this idea?
   - Who needs this idea? Do they need it now?
   - Can you fund this idea on your own?
   - If you had the money, would you fund this idea?

CHAPTER 15

Keys to Community Engagement as an Artist

Part of my faculty privileges at Juilliard is that we get a chance to attend several sessions at the beginning of the year for the students and faculty. There, we are fortunate to have Wynton Marsalis as our artistic director facilitating these meetings. He is such a wise spirit and champion for the music. This year, he spoke about community impact and engagement as an artist, and began to charge our students with several thoughts that I want to share with you.

- *"It is necessary for artists to desire to be both artistic, and a leader."*
- *"It is necessary for artists to have clarity and fire."*
- *"It's important to have constructive engagement as an artist."*

I love this approach and advice because it has less to do with being an artist and more to do with fully connecting with the community at large. This is something I not only believe in, but will dive into here in this chapter because I want to bring you here as well.

First, my backstory: If you would have told me years ago that so much of my life and work would be centered around community engagement and connection, I would have smiled and asked, "Really?" I say that not because I don't enjoy it, but because as an artist, we often think the biggest way that we will have impact in the world is solely through the display of our art. My perspective of community engagement began at church, where my family and I were always involved. This community was close and embracing and, in fact, never felt like a huge community because I knew everyone.

My next experience with the community was when I moved to New York City. There, we started to create educational partnerships that allowed us to venture to various neighborhoods and introduce jazz to them via master classes and workshops.

Now, through my work in the community, I realize that nothing is more powerful for people than connecting through art. Also, having the ability to make your art reach those who may not have necessarily even cared about art shows the true test and power of your artistry. For example, when I have a chance to perform or play for people who haven't been exposed to the music, it's a huge thrill for me. Many times, they will come up to me and give me true heartfelt feedback about their experience, and, when I'm especially lucky, I've created a new fan of the music.

SERVING THE COMMUNITY WITH ARTISTRY

Before Don't Miss a Beat (DMAB), our family was incredibly active via our community efforts in church. We functioned in a couple of different capacities at church, running Sunday school, vacation Bible school, planning Easter and Christmas theatrical productions, as well as the youth choir. Also, administratively, much of my family financially supported and sustained the growth of several churches.

When my family realized that there was a huge need for activity and mentorship for youth in Jacksonville, we decided we should form a business/organization. As devoted members of the church and community at large, we wanted to work to solve some issues, including the problem of crime being committed by so many young inactive teens. We wanted to contribute to the solution. We thought, "Let's build something that we can own and can build a legacy on as we help others to create a new life and journey." And we did.

As mentioned previously, I had no idea that this would be the work that I would do in my life. When we began DMAB, I was twenty-five years old and just a few years removed from college, and though I wasn't sure of my future plans, I didn't imagine that this would become the focus of my career.

However, I was given what I like to call, "the blessing of a burden," and the burden was for the community. I was no longer satisfied serving myself and my own artistic efforts; I wanted to contribute to something much larger than my own selfish pursuits. I had what I also like to call "a mirror talk," and what that became for me was an experience with my own spiritual purpose and an honest moment where I felt internally that I needed to give to these children. I heard and felt a voice within say, "The more you give to the children, the more the universe will conspire, and give you everything you need."

So, I began focusing on *my children*, and the organization in Jacksonville. While I was still working on my artistry, it was no longer the sole focus of my life. As I did that and started learning how to interface with the community, humble myself, and take pride in serving them, I felt—and still feel—that the universe has taken care of every desire and dream I have ever had.

Now dear students, I share this tale for three reasons: One, so you can better understand where I'm coming from; two, so that you can see that you never know what can happen (and I'm saying this in the most positive sense); and three, I encourage you to get involved with your own communities. The benefits, as I'm recounting here, are immeasurable both to them—and to you.

THE COMMUNITY CAN FEEL YOUR INTENTIONS

Working with the community is not only greatly rewarding, it's also humbling.

One of the first things I had to do as an artist with community engagement was to drop talk of all my achievements, and basically toss them to the wind, so to speak. A lot of these people don't even care about what you have accomplished; they have real needs—immediate basic needs. I had to be willing to take on a new identity; my community started to know me as "Mr. Owens," the guy who wants us to become something great. That's all, though now they have found out, primarily through social media, about all of the other work I do.

Still, I've worked hard to keep it separate so that they can really feel that I am here for them, and nothing else matters to me. When I adopted this attitude of focus on them, and started rolling up my sleeves, they began to see me as a brother, an advocate, and a person who loved them deeply. Through our work—and artistry—we began, together, to make growth and major positive changes.

SUPPORTING AND DEVOTING YOURSELF TO AN ASPECT OF COMMUNITY WORK

When we first started this work, my family tithed into it with our own money. This increased with time, and, in fact, I still consistently financially give to the work. In your case, if you're considering this—and I urge you to—depending on the scope of work you desire to do within the community, you will have to invest your time, energy, and possibly resources.

I have met several other colleagues, like Jessica Garand with Community Music Project, who have done something very similar in New York City. For example, Jessica offers orchestra and lessons for string instruments to kids from *at-hope* communities.

There are so many other wonderful programs that are in the world, doing great work. Behind them, you'll often find people who are sacrificing and giving of themselves for the pure satisfaction of giving back to the community.

So, to any creative who is considering doing community work, you need to check your intentions by asking yourself these questions:

1. Why are you doing this work?
2. If no one ever recognizes you, will you still remain committed to the work?
3. How can you attach your artistry to the agenda of the community?
4. How can you use your resources for the community?

5. How much sweat equity are you willing to put in?
6. Are you looking for the community to compensate you?

ALL YOU HAVE TO DO IS CARE

I once heard on a podcast from a really successful entrepreneur that one of the greatest keys to success is simply caring.

When you care deeply, there are amazing things that your care will attract to your business and ideas. The level of forward movement will be guaranteed, I believe, because when you care, others notice, and this can motivate them to join the cause. Many desire to help; they just need direction or a cause to inspire their efforts.

WHERE CAN YOU GO IF YOU'D LIKE TO START?

Start near you: look around in your own neighborhood, city, or nearby.

Additionally, there are several organizations and companies that exist to help artists who have a community agenda and can also figure out how to launch companies and organizations.

I am listing a small fraction of the national organizations that will be helpful and can lead to other organizations that can help with this mission:

- Americans for the Arts
- Chamber Music America
- Creative Capital
- Doris Duke Charitable Foundation
- Grammy Foundation
- Jazz Foundation of America
- Mid Atlantic Arts Foundation
- Music Cares
- National Art Education Association
- National Assembly of State Arts Agencies
- National Association of Latino Arts and Culture

- National Endowment for the Arts
- New England Foundation for the Arts
- New York Foundation for the Arts
- South Arts

Reflections for thought and discussion:

1. What about this chapter on community engagement spoke to you?
2. Is there someone you know personally who is devoted to community? What about an artist you've read or heard about?
3. As discussed in this chapter, some of the most dynamic and impactful ways to use your artistry is through community efforts. Is that something you have experienced? Is it something you'd like to experience?
4. What are parts of your artistry that you feel you could contribute through community engagement?

Reflections for writing:

1. What do you think could be your strong points as far as community contribution? List at least three of them here.
2. Write the name and actions of at least three people in your community who are making a difference and what they're doing.
3. Think about your own community involvement, and write a tentative plan for your possible interaction. Use these questions as a guide for writing.
   - Whom could you work with (both your audience/students and potential teammates)? What would you do?
   - How could you set it up?
   - How much time could you devote?
   - When would you start?

CHAPTER 16

The Mental Side of Being a Musician

"You cannot have a positive life and a negative mind."
—Joyce Meyer, Author, Speaker, and President of Joyce Meyer Ministries

We've touched on so many very important areas related to the music business, but we've neglected one that is equally important: mental health. One of the key drivers of being a better musician can also be the place of great challenges. Joyce Meyer, the great motivational and spiritual leader and writer whom I've quoted above, wrote a book many years ago called *The Battlefield of the Mind*. Within this book, she talks about how the mind is the place where some of the greatest wars are fought and won, and about how what the world experiences externally from us comes from the mind.

First, a short story:

Some time ago, I was teaching a private drum lesson, and during this lesson, so many things were brought to my attention about being a musician that I had not previously considered.

During this lesson, I saw that the student had no physical limitations as far as what he could play on the drum kit. However, his physical fluidity was limited because of his mental state.

I took the time to explain what I observed to the student, and once we acknowledged this obvious challenge he was having, we were able to re-approach the exercise, and the student began to excel beautifully on the drums.

What I learned that day was that the clearer you are mentally, the more ease you will be able to have on your instrument. Two key points I want to bring to your attention here:

- In additional to the physical aspects, being a musician requires a lot of mental focus and conditioning.
- Many times, the challenges that you are having techni- cally as a musician arrive because of a mental block borne from a combination of personal and musical insecurities.

To elaborate—as musicians, we must take time to feed our minds with positivity. I would even suggest what has worked for me: take the time to analyze your mind and where the problem began. Most of the time, in my case, the problem was present prior to my picking up my sticks. Unfortunately, the problem was re-triggered once I started playing. Once I had them in hand, the self-doubt accompanied me and I started simply going through the motions instead of playing and supporting the musicians as I should have been. This lack of focus was detrimental not only to my work, but to my colleagues' as well. As Steve Turre, one of the world's preeminent jazz innovators, trom- bonists, and seashellists told me many years ago, "Ulysses, who you are as a person comes through your instrument whether you want it to or not." For this reason and all the others, we need to be able to be present when we're onstage.

How did I resolve these triggered and non-present situations? Well, I have had to learn through the years how to quickly shut out self-doubt. I needed to figure out how to let the negativity not take root in my mind. I learned how to lower—and eventually silence—the naysayer voice within, and to channel my inner positive and encour- aging voices.

Mental health is a real thing, and as musicians, it's something we must invest in continually. In fact, next to fully developing our talent physically on our instruments, the most important task is to come up with mental strategies that can assist us. I heard someone say years ago that there is a voice on each side of our shoulders speaking to us: one speaking positively and the other speaking negatively. Depending on which one you're listening to you, your thoughts will be channeled in that direction. I actively work hard to allow positive voices of inspiration and affirmation to dominate my mind.

Musicians, we must make time to clear the mental pathways so beautiful music can be created from us and empower the audience that anxiously awaits to hear us.

It's important for me within this book to really provide a full-circle approach to what it takes to have a level of forward motion within your creative life, and that, dear students, starts with the mind.

DEPRESSION

When we talk about mental health and care, it's important to also touch on the topic of depression.

I want to speak about depression, because it's impossible to talk about happiness and peace without discussing depression, which for the artist, and especially the touring musician, is possible to encounter. Also, when you have burdens, goals, and time constraints within which you have to accomplish certain things, there is a certain level of isolation that you must experience to pursue your goals. This isolation can drift into depression. Again, taking a break can help. Of course, as I've recommended professionals to help you in other realms, you may need one in your case. However, only you can measure the severity of your feelings and, please, if you are feeling helpless, contact someone—a professional therapist—who can help you.

CONSULT WITH A THERAPIST OR COUNSELOR

Continuing on the theme of contacting a therapist, here is a bit of my backstory.

I remember that within one year, I lost a dear friend who was like a brother to me, I had to move due to major financial difficulties, and a romantic relationship that was incredibly dear to me ended. One day, I was watching a commercial about depression, and it stated that if you have experienced the loss of family members or significant others through death, moving, breakup, or divorce, you should seek therapy. Having experienced all of those traumatic events in less than six months, I realized it was time to find a therapist.

Growing up in a very spiritual and frequent church-going home, we were taught to take our problems to the creator and not to go to counseling unless it got really bad. It wasn't until I got to college that I met friends who had therapists most of their lives, and who described how that assistance was greatly helpful to their mental health.

However, back to that really tough moment—I decided to seek out a therapist, and I asked one of my close friends to give me a referral. That started the journey of therapy for me that has lasted for many years. It took a while for me to find the right therapist, one whom I connected with and who understood how to help me get through my own mental, spiritual, and emotional challenges. I have to tell you that I wouldn't be half the person or musician I am now if I hadn't had consistent therapy.

My therapist gave me strategies and mental tools that I use every day to overcome the challenges that life has set for me.

A therapist is necessary, especially for us as artists, because we are healers to our audiences, so we must be healed first before we can help others.

If you, dear student, have never met with a therapist, take the time and find one. It may take time, but make sure the therapist is the right fit for your style of counseling and communication so that you can best benefit from the healing power of talking things through with a professional.

OVERCOMING FEAR AND STAYING FOCUSED

"Fear is evolved to faith when men and women become reliant on the divine rather than social intervention."—Iyanla Vanzant, Inspirational Speaker, Lawyer,

New Thought Spiritual Teacher, Author, Life Coach, and
Television Personality

As Iyanla Vanzant points out in this quote, one of the most crippling
emotional mechanisms in this life that can block our progress is fear.
In my work as a creative, and also with children, I have often witnessed how fear gets in the way of my students' being able to perform
at the highest level of their artistic potential.

I have a child at my camp who has the voice of an angel, though
she has never trained nor really worked on it; it's just simply a gift.
One of the biggest hurdles my team and I are having to jump right
now is getting her not to be afraid of singing. Think about this:
she has a voice of an angel, and everyone recognizes it, but she is
afraid to open her mouth, not because of what is real, but due to
negative thoughts in her mind, and her being fully unaware of her
talent.

Many of us are like that student, with ideas that could really bring
the peace and resolve in the world that it needs—music within you
that is exactly what the radio is missing, film ideas that will bring
joy and peace to families, or knowledge to this society about important matters. Some of you also have book ideas that communities are
waiting on that will activate their minds and actions in a whole new
light. Yes, thankfully, there are ideas upon ideas. But if they are being
blocked by past failures and thus current fears, we won't benefit from
hearing from you—and you won't benefit from sharing.

Fear is debilitating to us all to a certain degree. I tell you that for
every success I have had, there have been failures and ideas that flat-
lined. Sometimes things just don't work out, but, dear students, pluck
that bad piece of fruit, don't cut down the whole tree.

I remember talking to one of my mentors who is really successful.
He started a business and put a lot of money into it; it was an amazing
venture. I remember visiting the business and it looked like something that was going to continue to thrive.

But when I saw him a few months ago, he told me how things had
changed. He said that he had been forced to close the business. I asked

him why. He said, "Initially it was a great idea, but it no longer is, so I needed to move in a different direction."

And then I asked him, "Do you feel like a failure?"

He said, "No, it just didn't work, so now it's time to discover what will."

I share his response because I think that it's a healthy one—despite feeling great pain and disappointment, he's moving forward; he's not letting the fear debilitate him.

Many of us, unfortunately, don't have his mental wherewithal—and we should. Fear creates these mountains in our mind and we perceive failure as a constant definition of who we are and what defines us.

That's not true, and it can't be true, because we have overcome so many other failures and setbacks.

A few things to realize about fear.

1. It is not real.
2. Fear is a mere feeling that seems real, and negatively impacts the perception of other real entities present in your life such as people, jobs, and places.
3. Fear can be conquered, but you have to replace it immediately with another powerful feeling.
4. Fear has no power to define you, or what you are desiring to create.
5. Fear only has the influence and power you give it.

So, I'm asking you to do something now. Remember this: today is the end of fear as you know it. Write it down in your phone, tablet, laptop or on paper. Put a time and date on it, and declare to your imagination and your mind that today is a new day, and the first day without fear being invited into the party of your life and mind.

We as human beings have full and creative license and agency to simply **be** in all the ways we want to be, so take it and enjoy it fully.

One of the most powerful lessons we can learn as human beings is that we are what we imagine for ourselves. We cannot be what we don't identify as, which is why we must be cautious about the adjectives and labels we attach to our personality. To say you are an overcomer is to also activate that you have the potential to overcome fear. But you will never have the potential for overcoming fear if you don't first identify as an overcomer.

My constant personal work is around the idea of always working on how to have more integrity and more patience. As mentioned before, in our field as creatives, who you are internally shows up on stage. The insecurity, the deceit, the fear, the confidence, hope, preparation all of it comes through. I also know that your internal strength is what will allow you to endure all the challenges in this business.

I have personally seen people succumb to all kinds of behaviors within the industry simply because they aren't patient enough or are refusing to work on integrity.

As one of my mentors says, "There is no traffic on the extra mile." Being patient also gives you a chance to fully develop your skill and simply wait to be recognized in the way you desire. But I have also continued to have to do a lot work around not waiting to or desiring to be recognized. The work is simply enough for me.

COMPARISON KILLS

To every one of you reading this book: I want you to never compare your journey to someone else's, because that can be the death of your motivation and progress in life and career. Having lived in NYC and been in business for a long time, I have met so many people who have become famous overnight, some who have gotten their due after many decades, and other combinations of success.

The goal is to focus on *you*, and understand fully what is expected of you in this life, and constantly seek to learn and love without ever separating those important characteristics from your journey. Always be willing to chart your own journey. Don't be afraid to do so.

This, dear students, has been something that helped me through every curveball: I have never subscribed to any pre-existing narratives that people had for me, and I always challenged them, because

it's not important for my success to even be explainable to everyone. I just want to remain in line with my purpose. Though yes,
we are different—you and I—in many ways, I am encouraging you
to adopt this attitude. Drop fear. Pick up your inner strength and
purpose.

PATIENCE TESTS MOTIVATION AND
PROVES INTEGRITY

"Integrity is who you are in the dark."—Alicia Olatuja,
Vocalist, Composer, and Arranger

I truly believe, as Alicia Olatuja says, that we are the person we are
when no one is watching. That—being who we are in the dark—is the
sum total of our humanity. It's important to make sure that *that* part
of us is fully vetted and challenged daily with actions of integrity.

I once heard a great speaker I mentioned previously, Dr. Matthew
L. Stevenson III, say that the best way to vet people is through the
process of time. When someone is waiting for something, you determine what their motivation is. This is easy for you to observe: the next
time you go somewhere really crowded, and there is a line, just look
at the people who are waiting to experience what they showed up for.
Also observe those who get impatient and walk away. This last group
was driven away—by themselves—because they just couldn't wait.

That's much like life; some people aren't fully motivated to have
what they desire, and many times, when things don't pan out the way
they want, they just give up, because they are frustrated with the timing of when it will happen. One of the interesting things to me about
timing is that it messes with our level of expectation, which then
messes with our ego and faith. I find that when I become at peace
with my own timing, I truly come to terms with God's plan as far
as timing for my life, and that leads me to release all of my failed
expectations.

When I am really motivated to do something, nothing will deter
me, not even waiting. We must make sure we really desire that which

we say we desire, and when timing becomes a probable reality, it's time to fasten the bootstraps and look forward to the ride and journey.

The difficult moments in my life always arise when life forces me to simply be patient and wait for the manifestation of what's ahead of me. It's funny that now, as I get older, I am starting to see some interesting patterns in my life. From the time I was about eighteen years old, every time I hit a new decade, my life seemed to kind of turn upside down and I went through some major transitions. These changes forced me to feel, think, be, and conduct myself differently.

When I was about eighteen, I was in the process of graduating from high school, and I remember that waiting on my college acceptance letter felt like sheer pain. I had done everything I was supposed to do, but I had to wait on life to reveal what destiny had already prepared for me.

Then, I remember when I was about twenty-seven, and my personal life I went through a lot of changes around starting Don't Miss a Beat with my family. I was commuting back and forth to Florida, and just trying to figure out what was next for me economically. I was working, but I didn't have a steady job that could completely sustain me. I had also just gone through a major relationship loss in my life and had to move on. All I felt was surrounded by instability, but I held fast to what I knew was destined for me.

Shortly after that time, I was greeted with a few new associations—those I had with Christian McBride and Kurt Elling. Those meetings changed the course of my life for the positive, and created much of what allows me to write this book for you today.

Even more recently, my life went through another major challenge, because as much as I love touring and playing music, I was feeling the tug to develop my writing and take the time off to fully throw myself into this work. Like earlier times, my life felt unstable, felt unclear, yet there was this light I could see at the end of the tunnel, and I had to just keep trusting my instincts, which have never failed me.

I mention these pivotal moments because what has sustained me is my commitment to my character and how I choose to treat people and honor them in the midst of my own struggles. I have never let a circumstance change how I approached someone or a situation; I am always seeking to give my best, no matter what.

Life is a full-circle journey, and many times, some of the key players you may be interacting with now may change roles later, and could impact your progress in the future. Treat everyone with grace, and humility. As Mulgrew Miller, my late mentor, used to always tell me when I first met him when I was just eighteen, "Ulysses, this is a funny business. You may even need to hire me for a gig one day." Funny enough, my career did go to a completely different place than it was when he first met me, and I was able to hire him for a gig. In conclusion, I say to you, honor everyone on your way up the ladder.

STAY THE COURSE AND HOLD ON TO YOUR DREAM

I want to share another example: I was literally almost done writing this book, and I was taking a drive when I began to think about the process of how this book started as an idea, then how I became inspired via conversations that this idea needed to be developed, and that what it needed was more focus.

Then I backtracked in my mind: I remembered how about two years ago, I only had a few paragraphs that summarized what the book could be about. I had even created an outline based on the book ideas that was also doubling as a structure for my lectures.

The thought came to start pitching the idea to publishers so I could potentially gain interest and funding to write this book. I reached out to a publisher thanks to my friend Chavon Sutton. The publisher said that though he thought the book was a great idea, based on what I submitted, it just wasn't ready and complete enough to be considered to be added to their roster. Nevertheless, he shared constructive insight that I have incorporated now—at this stage—to finish this book.

Also, at that time, I applied to various sources that could potentially have funded the book.

However, despite my great desire to do this project, things were not looking like they were working with me. Publishers were not interested in taking it to the next level, and funding didn't come through. At that point, I honestly thought that maybe writing the book was just not in the cards.

So I started lecturing, and the more I lectured, the more I encountered a community of people who needed to hear the perspective that I was offering around the music business. More importantly, I was enjoying my ability to encourage them not to stop pursuing their dreams, and how to take steps to make their goals a reality. That, in essence, was the dream behind this book project. I began to do the work, then I met Arlen Gargagliano, and we decided to create a small workbook to accompany my lectures. Once we made that decision, I reached out to a publisher I had been in touch with previously, who asked if I was interested in submitting the book for consideration. Within three months, I worked with Arlen, completed the book proposal, and submitted it to the publisher—and got a book deal.

Dear students, timing is such a key component in our lives. If we remove our idea of time and separate it from the idea of success, we can reach greater heights. For example, if you study any great CEOs, celebrities, or successful individuals, there is always a period of time—uncontrolled by them—when they had to wait for certain things to come to fruition. I share this with you along with a request for you to try to be patient. Be hungry, but patient. I meet artists all the time who want projects, albums, and opportunities to just fall in their laps, but have no level of patience and trust in time. The latter is what is needed.

FOCUS YOUR TIME AND ENERGY

Another reality for me was that I needed to take the time to commit myself to writing this book. Many times, we want opportunities, but part of timing and acquiescing to it adds a different level of challenge. Because of the nature of my life and how things can be really busy, I constantly have to be sensitive to the reality of timing, to recognize when it was time to commit and focus on a goal I had set for myself.

I now look at my writing, my life, and my career. I am writing and completing this book. To be honest, I thought I needed a fancy fellowship, or job position, or even a publisher to let me know that I could write a book. I had to simply take the time to form the vision and plan, and once I took the steps towards writing, all of what I thought I needed began to form around the first steps I took to make this a reality. There were also several events in my life that occurred to confirm that this is the time, I am the person, and that I am mentally and spiritually ready.

There are so many things that need time to develop, and we can only force or encourage things to a certain point. Sometimes we need to let things be, at least for a bit. If we can carry on, go to bed and wake up every day, our life, minds, and spirits will continue to grow.

So, here's a bit more time advice: Don't rush the process to be ready. Do what you can do, but also find other things to keep your mind focused, and maybe even distracted in a healthy way, so you can properly wait for those things to be fully developed within for your future. It's better to show up ready, than unready. Why? Because lack of preparedness will cost you more than just being upset and impatient. It can, in some ways, even cost you your life.

KEEP YOUR EYE ON THE PRIZE

I remember when I moved to New York City, I met Eric Reed, and I asked him, "How long do you think it takes a musician to make it?" He responded that he felt it takes about five professional years in New York City to really get into a flow of the scene, have consistent work, and start to make a name for yourself.

I don't disagree with him, because though I moved to NYC for college, and started touring a bit in college, once I graduated, I felt like I was starting over. Once I finished school, my reputation had to be built upon my own musicianship and relationships separate from those I had in college. I had to make my own name.

Fast forward to now—about twenty years later. After being here that long, and considering the relationships that I have been able to maintain and grow, the reality is that some relationships came to be once I put in the time. Now people can vouch for my talent because I have been here long enough. This brings me back to staying power. This has to be an integral part of the equation of success: time is a key component in success.

WHAT IS YOUR PRIZE?

In the song "Keep your Eye on the Prize," the lyrics encourage the audience to keep their eyes on the prize in the context of both the song and the reality of the African-American struggle. That prize is freedom: freedom to exist, have access to education, resources, and the inalienable rights that all should be born and raised with.

For you or me, our *prize* may be completely different. After all, we are different, and we all have internal goals and desires that tie to results that we feel are an adequate representation of our hard work. No one else can determine that prize for ourselves but you and I.

We have to be clear what the prize is for us. Once we figure that out, we shouldn't take our eyes off of it.

For me, the prize was being able to live life on my own terms and constantly be associated with projects that are in tandem with my purpose. I want to constantly produce high-quality work that is timeless and impactful. Obviously, recognition, increased compensation, and notoriety are all the collateral that comes with the prize.

HOLD ON

As author and inspirational speaker Connor Beaton wisely states, "Aim for fulfillment and success will follow." Aiming for fulfillment means working towards what you want to happen. It doesn't—as previously discussed—just happen. It's not enough to keep your eye on the prize; one must hold on to the dream associated with the prize. Get that idea of success in your mind and simply gaze at it, and don't let it out of your sight. Now hold on to it and don't let go.

Remember: an idea gets rejected not because it's not fundamentally sound, but because no one in top management will personally benefit from its success. Hold on, and make it happen.

Reflections for thought and discussion:

1. Look back at the opening quote of this chapter: *"You cannot have a positive life and a negative mind."* What does this mean to you? Explain with an example.

2. Have you ever seen a performer—or even had a teacher— who was physically there but mentally not present? How did you know that he or she was not "all in" as far as what he or she was doing?

3. How do you attain mental focus?

4. This chapter addressed the point that fear often holds us back. What are your fears as far as your artistry?

Reflections for writing:

1. List three things standing in the way of you being the best you.

2. List your biggest fears on a piece of paper, ball them up, and set them on fire (in a safe location!), and as they burn, let them dissipate from your mind and your life.

3. We talked in this chapter about keeping an eye on the prize. What's your prize? Write it down (it may be a word, several words, or even a paragraph).

CHAPTER 17

The Emotional Side of Being a Musician

There is, obviously, a huge overlap between the mental and emotional sides of being a musician, but—and stay with me here—this is just as important. Of course there is an overlap, but by mental, as mentioned in the last chapter, I'm referring primarily to mindset and your ability to process information. In this section, I talk more about what you can do to foster your happiness and thus emotional success. Now, dear students, note that I am not saying that you should ignore other emotions; I would never say that. But, as always, I think, it's a balance. Happiness has to weigh well in your emotional world.

FEED YOUR HAPPY

Part of the mental side of being a musician is not only creating and reaching for—working for—your goals, it's also about taking care of yourself.

Happy people let themselves experience success and self-recognition. It's important for your aim in this life and pursuit of artistic freedom to pursue peace and happiness as part of your ultimate goal. After all, despite the history of the tortured artist syndrome that has radiated for many decades, that's not the life that I desire to have. And, frankly, no one wants to experience life as a miserable artist. It's a choice to have a fulfilling life that involves both spiritual and internal wholeness and thus happiness.

Again, it's important that you care for YOU. Make sure that you identify activities that feed your happy and allow you to expand your world with a mindset that allows you to thrive. Someone told me a while ago that what you think about expands—so if you think about failure, it will also expand. Think about success, and it will expand.

And speaking of success and happiness, you want to keep in mind all the things that make you content—and use them!

Here are the activities that feed my happy:

- Having a meal with my family
- Having a meal with my dear friends
- Engaging in the most in-depth conversation with a similar minded individual
- Sitting and people-watching outside while taking in a cool breeze
- Eating a great meal
- Going to a museum
- Enjoying a dance show
- Meditating
- Writing

TAKING A BREAK

Sometimes, when we're in the middle of so much, we need to just step back, take a look, and appreciate or reevaluate.

I was speaking to my manager a few years ago, and I was really stressed out because the things I felt should have happened simply had not occurred yet in my career, and as a result of that, I was so disappointed. And, actually, I was kind of ready to throw in the towel on an idea.

My manager stopped me. He said, "Ulysses, I can tell you are frustrated, but I don't think you have looked at the victories we have accomplished." He began to talk about the things that have happened for me in my career. Sometimes, even though I am accomplishing things, because I am constantly seeking to be better, it's important for me to figure out how to take a break and look at my successes and victories. I encourage you to do the same.

My mind is very detailed and so addicted to the detailed results that I want that if what is materializing doesn't look exactly like that, it can cause a lot of frustration. Taking a break allows me to just focus on something else and really meditate and breathe in and be thankful for what has materialized and become. So, yes, we all need to take breaks and reflect.

AN EMPTY SOUL CREATES EMPTY MUSIC— EMBRACE PERSONAL RELATIONSHIPS

During the time of writing this book, I considered the idea of touching on personal and romantic relationships. Of course, these types of relationships play fundamental roles in our lives, but I wasn't sure if this would pertain to guidance as far as helping you with your career.

So, initially, I sought to avoid this topic here. But then I thought about how so many times, having love in my life taught me and added much to my musical and career pursuits. Also, many younger students and artists have flooded my inbox and called me constantly about how to navigate their own relational challenges in the midst of their music. I've even heard from some people who are having challenges within relationships and marriages and need guidance for knowing how to deal with that in the midst of creating art.

This brought me to my conclusion: if I am going to really create a guide, I need to deal with every facet that affects us as musicians and creatives. In the spirit of not leaving any stone unturned, I want to speak about a few vantage points of relationships romantically, and how to manage them in the midst of your career pursuits as a musician and creative.

Having a partner

One of the greatest joys of my life is when I am in a beautiful romantic relationship; it just makes life great. Everything makes sense, the birds hum differently, the clouds look brighter, and it just feels great to know that you have someone with who you can share your life with. I also know that the quality and level of a relationship that I will be able to have boils down to the quality of the relationship that I have with myself.

People are in relationships with themselves first. Now stay with me here: you first need how to have a relationship with yourself. For instance, it took me along time to learn how to be alone. Actually, it took years. My family would laugh at me because I was always so driven by having people around me.

However, once I started to find my passion and purpose, I started to love being alone, and I was also much easier to be in relationship with because I understood myself better and could communicate that to my partner. In my early relational years, I was a bit needy and it would frustrate my partners as far as how much I would require from them. Once I learned to access that love and attention from myself, and my own spiritual relationship, I was able to enjoy that person for who they were, while not depending on them to fulfill me or affirm my identity. Now, ironically, people say that I like to be alone too much! Still, I know I'm a much better partner for it.

The right partner

Being in a relationship is challenging for anyone, but when you have the right partner, one who will be committed to a journey with you, and one with whom you can also commit, then you have the ideal combination.

Some people may ask, "Well, how do you know that person is the right partner?"

And to that I have to say: Let your instincts tell you. I think you will know when it feels right, and when it feels wrong, Listen to yourself.

I was in the middle of getting to know someone romantically at one point, and in our conversations, she spoke about a previous relationship. She explained that during the time of that relationship, she was embarking upon a new type of career choice, and her previous mate was not supportive at all of her new artistic desires. In fact, her previous partner criticized her choice to change career paths. As a result, even when we were getting to know each other, she still carried a large amount of hurt around the situation. Clearly, this had not been the right person for her.

I bring this to your attention because I know that many of you reading this book may have people in your life who aren't the right people for you, also. I think it's helpful if you have people in your life who challenge you and ask you why you choose something, but ultimately, they should support you with love and patience, and respect your goals and ambitions.

Lastly, anyone who decides to be with an artist must understand that they will forever share you with your first love: your art. Most people enjoy what they do, but we as artists, in many ways, are our art. It takes a very special and mature soul to know how to love someone like that. Relationships should help you be a better you, not get in the way of you being you. With creative minds, we also need space to be moody, creative, and undefined—and not always knowing what direction we are headed in. The right partner will know how to support you through both the creative and the challenging moments.

Self-sufficient and fulfilled partner

Your partner should have something that is important to him or her; this should be something that gives inner strength and drives him or her. This way, your partner can identify with you. Your partner must be secure, and have something that makes their heart sing. Otherwise, your partner will constantly impede your moment and in some cases be jealous of the connection you have to your craft.

It can be challenging when you are with a partner in a relationship totally based on you: where you are their world. This is because, after all, your world is the music and other things, and not focused solely on your partner. There is a really great book that helped me called *Wholeness*, by Touré Roberts. He speaks very candidly about everyone seeking to be their whole selves individually, as opposed to together. He says, in talking about relationships, "Two halves cannot make a whole."

Some of the greatest relationships that I have seen in the business have worked when each partner brings their whole self to the relationship.

Timing is everything

Even as I write this book, I am currently not in a romantic relationship, and it's not because I don't desire to be in one. During this year of my life, I have written two books, moved to a different city, and maintained multiple business pursuits and obligations. Honestly, I tried to have a relationship with several potential partners, but it didn't work for a myriad of reasons. Some people felt they weren't ready to share their life, and wanted to solely focus on their career. Others felt a little overwhelmed by my life and the journey that I am on, and others simply weren't interested.

I state this as a reality to speak to the fact that timing is everything in life. As mentioned previously, to develop at various stages of life, you need time alone so that everything can come into fulfillment with minimal distractions. But there is a time and place for everything, and I have learned to find contentment with where I am and not seek to superimpose my own desires on what actually should be occurring in my life, along with who is supposed to be in my life as well.

Be equally yoked

I am a man of faith, and in scripture, it speaks about being unequally yoked, though I don't want to use this book to preach or tie anyone to any specific religion, because that's not my goal. That phrase of being equally yoked has always been fundamental to me. It ties into even how I choose my team, friends, and every relationship that is in my life. I believe when you join in relationships with people, they need to be equal, and bring what you bring in a different manner. It's my belief also that as an artist, we are vessels of creativity, and we were placed in this life and on this planet to heal people through music and our creativity. With that understanding, we have to really be careful about who we allow near our energy, because people can bring in negative energy and it can restrict and interrupt the flow of our creativity.

Also, it's important to know that as artists, our talent draws masses of people to us and sometimes who we draw may not always match who will be aligned with our lives and destiny.

You are not just anyone as an artist, and you should make sure you behave as such and create boundaries as far as who you allow in your life and near you. My father used to always tell me, "Son, you aren't better than anyone, but know that you are different, and take care of yourself because of that knowledge." I pass his words of wisdom on to you.

My hope is that all of you reading this utilize some of these points regarding the alignment of your personal and romantic life. If you are single, and looking for a partner, I encourage you to continue radiating positivity and you will find someone who will work alongside you and contribute spark and wellbeing.

BE HUNGRY FOR MORE

In closing this chapter, I want to share another story with you.

I met this incredibly talented student from Tel Aviv, Israel, named Elay Kadosh, who plays bass. He wrote a beautiful email to me telling me how much he loved my playing and that he wanted to study with me when he visited New York City. He arrived in New York City, and at our first lesson, I asked him who else he planned to study with while he was here. He listed about ten other amazing musicians, some of the top call players in town. I asked him how he could afford such a thing, and he told me has been saving money for over a year to come to NYC and study with these musicians. He told me that his father also helped to make this happen by assisting him financially. I was completely moved by Elay's dedication and drive.

While Elay was here, he got a chance to study with the legendary Ron Carter, who is very particular about the students he chooses to teach; he wants to make sure that they are ready to work with the level of focus he desires to teach with. I asked him how in the world he managed to do that. He explained that he wrote Ron a three-page letter about his mission, and why he just had to see him and study with him while in NYC. The result? He ended up with not one but two lessons from Ron Carter.

Elay's heart and humanity has moved me tremendously. Part of this is just because I got to witness his pure strength and drive. But it's also because he reminded me so much of my own inner hunger.

Understand that if you want something bad enough, you will get it if you fight for it. Most of us don't have what we desire because we simply don't want it bad enough. There is part of our inner being that is satisfied with where we currently are, and that's why our situation hasn't and won't move.

I believe the Universe has a way of acknowledging that which we feel we can't live without. For most of the success and forward motion that we seek, there is something inside of us that can live without it, and that's why we are living without it.

I want to live a life of purpose, and I also want to be a person of excellence, which is why everything that I seek to do comes from that place, and I am uncompromising about that.

Looking at students like Elay, I know that his dreams will continue to come true in time, because he is hungry for more and will stop at nothing to have it.

And so, dear students, I urge you to work for what your inner being tells you to be or have. Don't let obstacles—and there will be obstacles, both inner and outer ones—deter you. In closing, I have three points for your consideration:

- **Feed the mind and the rest will follow**: Keep yourself educated, well read, and well versed in what's going on around you and in the world. We musicians are focused on our art, of course, but also need to broaden our minds in other arenas.
- **Make time to also study others**: There are so many wonderful and admirable people who came before you. Take the time to learn about them, and how they did what they did. We can learn so much from our elder, more experienced musicians—and from our colleagues, too.

- **Toughen your mental hide:** Become okay with criticism, and also understand where it's coming from. We are in the public eye, and being there is a privilege, but can also be, at times, a burden. We hear all kinds of comments—good and bad. Take note of what you hear, but don't take it all to heart; it can build you up, but it can also damage you.

Many times, as musicians, our idea of success extends to something that is about posting and proving to others how successful we are. However, the true measure of success in my book is your level of skill and ability to advance forward in your career.

You know that you have talent. Now, almost at the end of this book, I want to enforce the translation of that talent into your success. Let's start by considering a school of thought that will point you in that direction:

8 PRINCIPLES OF TURNING YOUR TALENT INTO SUSTAINED SUCCESS

1. You have to start.
2. Be clear about your goals.
3. Be exceptional at your talent.
4. Pursue mastery.
5. Create a team of advisors that will give you truth and helpful advice.
6. Finish what you started.
7. Have faith in your ideas.
8. Leave room for divine intervention and direction.

NO ROAD MAP FOR SUCCESS

Here is the reality: you can read this book and follow every instruction, yet nothing may go as planned, because life is what you intend it to be.

I had a conversation with my friend Alicia, and we spoke about the reality that our life is the sum total of several elements: what decisions we actually make, what we have or will have, what we work towards, and what we subconsciously and innately desire.

The question is, how can you bring this all together?

There is truly no road map for success, and as a person who has read many biographies and listened to tons of podcasts about people's lives, every journey is completely different. Most people never expected to be where they are, and guess what? Some people absolutely planned and expected to be where they are. It's all different. Even if we think we can explain it, we can't.

BE CONFIDENT

As James Norman, founder and CEO of Pilotly says, "You have to possess an ignorant amount of confidence to be a successful entrepreneur." As we've touched on, trusting in yourself and being confident are huge factors in your success. During this walk, probably one of the most difficult things for me, personally, was to maintain my confidence in the midst of insurmountable odds, and what felt like rejection and defeat.

But confidence is about clinging onto a higher level of belief in your identity, and from that identity comes your purpose.

THE GIFT OF BEING A MUSICIAN

Being a musician professionally is a choice, yet being given the gift to play music is a true privilege and honor. If you have made it to the end of this book, and are taking the time to digest all of the thoughts, challenges, and reflections, I want you to now meditate on the honor of being a musician.

It's a gift to be a creative individual. I realize some who might be reading this book may just love being creative and finding time in your life to embrace your creative genius and power.

In my case, there were times of transition and challenges when it didn't feel like it was a gift. This was primarily because the love and calling that I have to be a musician sometimes generated more pain, confusion, anxiety, and angst.

But what I clung to, and continue to hold fast to, is my love of music. At two years old, I fell in love with music, not the business, strategy, nor branding. I fell in love with that feeling and accepted the God-given ability to perform and express myself through music. A gift is something that is given to you, and you appreciate it.

My father told me many years ago, "Son, never give away a gift someone gives to you, because that person wanted you to have what they gave you."

God gave me music, and many of you reading this book were given a gift, which is what made you curious enough to pick up this book and read it to empower and better yourselves.

Never regret the gift, nor forfeit it. Figure out how to navigate it and improve yourself, but never forget that your creative genius is a gift. Surrender yourselves fully to it, and everything will work out for your good.

Reflections for thought and discussion:

1. Now that you're almost at the end of this book, what does being a successful musician mean to you?
2. How can you advise a musical artist as to how to build confidence (in general)?
3. How can you help yourself be more confident?
4. How do you feel about the role of romantic relationships in your life right now?
5. How can you work to toughen your mental hide?

Reflections for writing:

1. What activities "feed your happy"? Write a list of five things that you most enjoy.
2. What concrete steps can you take based on the eight principles of turning your talent into sustained success? Write

at least one example of how you can achieve/reach for each
of these principles.

- You have to start.
- Be clear about your goals.
- Be exceptional at your talent.
- Pursue mastery.
- Create a team of advisors that will give you truth
  and helpful advice.
- Finish what you started.
- Have faith in your ideas.
- Leave room for divine intervention.

3. We talked in this chapter about keeping an eye on the
   prize. What's your prize? Write it down (it may be a word,
   several words, or even a paragraph).

CHAPTER 18

A Musician's Mastery

Well, dear students, at this point you have committed to reading this book in its entirety. I wanted this last chapter to be the missing link as far as what your career is yearning for.

While many of you are very much under way in your career, you may still be in a place where you are trying to figure out how to have what you desire. Mastery may be the missing link to your puzzle of success and purpose.

WHAT IS MASTERY?

It's described as having a comprehensive knowledge in an area or skill. However, in my opinion, mastery is an undeniable level of power and talent in an area. When someone is a master, and you have the privilege of listening and observing that master, you are left in awe; that skill is so dazzling, so profound, that it renders bystanders speechless—and delighted.

Mastery—in any field—leaves people in awe and without questioning; there's a definitiveness on the part of mastery. When you have the honor of watching a master chef, and see how she or he creates by instinctively combining spices and ingredients, you don't question his or her ability to do so.

I feel the same rings true for a master musician in my field of jazz. You don't question if John Coltrane can play the horn, or if Charlie Parker gets the concept of sound, or if Herbie Hancock has virtuosity.

They do it—seemingly effortlessly. And watching a master at work is a rare treasure.

What I love the most about people who are masters at what they do is that they do it with such ease; there's a smooth ebb and flow in all they do, because they were destined to do it.

What is sad to me is that my generation has lost the idea and even desire to be a master. What we have fallen in love with is attention, and if you gain enough attention, it's assumed that you have achieved mastery. So, you have many people seeking to become actors, musicians, singers, visual artists, designers, etc., and they have never fully studied and embodied their craft. They have posted several videos and gained some followers, but their followers are also not in pursuit of mastery. The sad consequence is the cyclical problem of a lot of mediocrity leading and expanding more mediocrity.

MASTERY STILL MATTERS

Contrary to what I'm seeing these days, I believe that mastery still matters. And I want you to believe this too, dear students.

As I've mentioned, you have to seek to be great to be great, otherwise you'll just settle for the comfort of mediocrity. The pursuit of mastery is necessary towards the path of sustained success, and it's virtually impossible without it.

MASTERY TAKES TIME

We've talked about patience before. Most things in this life will not happen in the timing that you think they should, but when all of the necessary parties and events are aligned, and you are actually ready within, it will happen—and with the right people to assist you.

There's something I used to hear years ago as a child in church, and I apply it now to my universal knowledge of understanding, the law of attraction, and the power of intention: a delay is not a denial. Some things will take a little bit of time because there is more within you that needs to be developed, or, as my mother would say, "More is involved in this process than you realized."

Also, you don't want success to come to the underdeveloped and unready part of you and your character, because then you won't be able to maintain it. Seeds grow from being consistently watered, and some aspects of growth are not always visible to the naked eye. The question is: Can you keep going when you feel growth but don't see it?

You can't be in a rush to be a master. When I was in Japan, I learned about the path of a sushi chef master. If you want to become a sushi chef, you have to work for a master chef for over ten years. That's a decade of cutting fish, cleaning up behind the chef, and just serving so that you can learn. I am pretty certain that within the first year the trainee may feel like he knows how to make sushi. I am sure in the second year these chefs are more confident at making sushi, and perhaps even running a restaurant. But after ten years of training, there is no question about their level of mastery, and beyond that, well, they are masters, and will spend the rest of their lives being masters in this area—and probably teaching others to join their ranks.

Celebrated author Malcolm Gladwell says that it takes about 10,000 hours to master a skill. Now, of course, those 10,000 hours will have to be subtracted from other parts of your life. They may be taken from your time to party, hang out, and pursue personal matters.

This book is not designed to present you with quick fixes to be successful; that is not my mission—nor has it been my journey. However, this guide will help you over time to focus on the right thing and pursue the right connections, manage the right relationships, and be informed on the path of mastery of your craft.

That's the beauty of mastery—that the years are not wasted. I spent over twenty years studying music, and even now I continue to study. Still, all of those years have continued to help me apply that same focus and understanding to other pursuits in my life—playing, teaching, writing, and more. Again, mastery takes time.

My question to those of you who want to turn your talent into sustained success is: What are you willing to do to make that happen?

The life of a master is not for just anyone, and if you want to truly be a unique voice in your industry, you have to pursue mastery with all of your might and heart. It means exhausting yourself and your talent.

My request is clear: I want all of you reading this book to pursue mastery at the highest level possible because it's rare, and beyond that, it will create demand around the category or focus of your mastery. I recognize that this can be challenging when you have multiple passions and gifts; however, you must surrender your craft to the pursuit of mastery.

Now that I am writing the end of this book, and you are reading it, there are a few things I ask you to consider.

I encourage all of you to:

- Go clearly into identifying your dreams.
- Go forward in the direction of them.
- Don't lose faith as you run towards the finish line.
- Don't stop until you cross that finish line.

Dear students, I hope this book is a tool that will help you navigate through the tunnel, to the light of your dreams. I wish you all all the best, now and always.

—U

AFTERWORD

Alexander Smalls

I'm proud to share this letter from Alexander Smalls, prolific author, restaurateur, and opera singer.

Dear Students,

Congratulations! I commend you for choosing this exceptional book to assist you in navigating the career challenges of an "up and coming" successful music career. Ulysses Owens, Jr.'s new book, *The Musician's Career Guide: Turning Your Talent into Sustained Success* is an inspiring and informative guide to help you make the most of your talent, ambition. and handiwork, which you will most certainly need so as to climb the ladder of success.

As a successful and dedicated professional who started a musical career as an opera singer, achieving both a Grammy and a Tony, I sympathize with you and the journey you face ahead. My training included studies at the University of North Carolina (known back then as NCSA), and the Curtis Institute of Music in Philadelphia. Unlike you, my career as an opera singer occurred in parallel, then was surpassed by, my career in the culinary arts. Today I add some additional accolades: award-winning chef, author, and award-winning restaurateur.

But the lessons I learned as a professional musician were fundamental in completing the perfect recipe for my culinary arts career. Those lessons you will most certainly find in this book.

An enormously talented and committed musician, Ulysses Owens Jr. is the consummate professional, and he wants to make sure you can be, too. He realized while studying and gigging—playing jobs, jamming with ultra-professionals—that there was so much more to becoming a professional musician than just being talented. Talent was just the beginning, as he notes in his book, but there was far more required to achieve the career he sought. Ulysses spent all of his energies developing a path to success he now wants to share with all of you.

Listen, I know the ups and downs, the demands of an artist's life, and the highs and lows, sacrifices made, lack of money and, at times, confidence. Believe me, a musician's life is not for the faint of heart.

But the good news is that, unlike me, you have the benefit of this amazing book from one of the most gifted, organized, positive, and hardworking musicians I know.

Take this to heart: you have the best coach you could ever hope for, and he has made it easy for you. It's all in this book.

Good luck . . . be prepared . . . be brilliant!

Alexander Smalls

THOUGHTS FROM OTHER SOURCES—ABOUT THE MUSIC INDUSTRY AND MORE

There is so much out there in this world for you, dear students, and I have enjoyed sharing lots of suggestions, ideas and answers to many of your questions related to your long and rich career as a professional musician.

As you've seen, I've woven a lot of recommendations into the pages of this book. When I spoke to some of my advisors and about this book, they also shared some relevant guidance with me. So here, dear students, are some small bites of advice from people that have helped me along my musical journey. After all, our journeys are never singular; they are always collective. The idea, of course, is to always keep the inspiration going!

On the topic of the future of the music industry for you as professionals in this field

Fredara Mareva Hadley, Ph.D., Ethnomusicology professor in the Department of Music History at Juilliard:

"Technology has changed so much about how music is produced and consumed. And we have a glut of music and content everywhere. But the music that moves us and truly connects with people still resonates. In an over-stimulated society people are still hungry to feel something. To hear truth. To be moved. We will always make room for that because no technology can synthesize that feeling."

Marcus and Jean Baylor, a.k.a. The Baylor Project, American jazz duo from New York City:

"Change happens very quickly in this business, especially now in the technology age. Being open to change will help you navigate new norms.

"Understanding that being creative applies to everything, not just music. Creativity applies to business, marketing, branding, publicity, literally every aspect of what you do. Creativity is your super power. Tapping into that on every level is your best defense against change."

On the topic of taking advantage of downtime

Myles Weinstein, President, Unlimited Myles, an exclusive booking agency representing some of the finest jazz artists today:
"Be as creative as you can be. For some, that can mean writing new music. For others, it could mean just taking this time to woodshed stuff you haven't had time to practice before."

On the topic of mental health for musicians

Courtney Bryan, Pianist and Composer:
"I consider myself to be an ambitious person. I just find it important for my ambition for career success to be in balance with pursuit of overall fulfillment. Because of my religious/ spiritual beliefs, this fulfillment is less a need to be 'happy' in a fleeting way, but to fulfill my main purpose—to create uninhibited beauty. This goes into art, relationships, social concerns, religious practices for me."

On the topic of the best advice received—about being a musician, and being successful

Also from Courtney Bryan:

"My mother gave me this advice: an artist's trajectory is not a linear process. Don't assume that your earlier works are less important and that you will create a magnum opus at the end of your life. She said each work we do is important and sometimes your great work(s) can come earlier in life. Some artists produce a large body of work for a long time. Some may produce one great work that impacts others, and not have a large body of work. And also, I've always paid attention to how there are sometimes clusters of productivity in a musician's career where (s)he/they produce a lot (or one major work), and there are other times we don't hear much about. It's natural to have valleys as well as mountains. Some people live a long time and some a short time. What that tells me is to put my all into each project, hoping for a long life and long career, but never taking the moment for granted."

Epilogue

At the time of my writing this book, we were dealing with the pandemic, COVID-19—which totally changed our lives in so many ways.

I lived in NYC during the devastating days of 9/11, and I distinctly remember that crisis affecting the artistic community. At that time, it was my first year in NYC, and I was in college. I thought the world was ending. However, I watched the artistic communities and the world rally together, and become more whole and united than they were before.

This—COVID-19—was different. At this time, no artists, no matter the genre, were able to tour or promote their music in the normal way. We had to completely shift and to discover a new relationship with our music and our audiences. I have seen artists have tours cancelled indefinitely, and I think what plagues us beyond losing relatives and colleagues to this horrific virus is wondering when we will be able to create again.

Wynton Marsalis is someone I have admired for many reasons. I respect his vision and foresight, and for this reason, I chose to quote some of his talk here. Though this talk was given in the time of corona, it's, as he is, both wise and timeless.

Wynton Marsalis, the prolific trumpeter and composer, director of Juilliard Jazz and the managing and artistic director of Jazz at Lincoln Center, contributed advice via *Skain's Domain: An Intimate Conversation with Wynton Marsalis.*

On staying inside

- Embrace the space and be healthy—in terms of discipline and how you handle the rest.
- Set long-term internal goals.
- Keep perspective.
- Organize your short-term goals and plan each day with a doable schedule.
- Diversify your day.
- Stay humorous: Joke, play around, and clown!
- Stay active in your mind and exercise.
- Hope and optimism are internal.
- You play for yourself first.
- Go internal to go external.

On community

- Reach for community.
- Create your community based on your interests and concerns, not based on geography.
- Get to know the people you're with.

On playing your instrument

- I don't separate technique from expression or the soul from the spirit.
- Accept that it [practicing] takes discipline. Then get to work. But put aside some time to not do anything, too.

On not having other musicians to play with

- When you have restrictions, you work inside that.
- Make the best of the situation.

On the desires that prevent young musicians from attaining mastery

- The desire to waste time.
- Needing recognition from peers.
- The desire to avoid insecurities.

On playing fast tempos

- Try to do things you can't do. Chart your progress. Tape yourself.
- For fast tempos, Dizzy told me to tap on 1 and 3, not 2 and 4.
- As musicians we're really dealing with our imagination and our ears.
- Get to the fundamental root of what your problem is.

On keeping perspective

- Look at what you get and be grateful for that, not looking at what you didn't get.

COVID-19 also gave me some relevant insights. After all, as mentioned throughout this book, most musicians and creatives are entrepreneurs by design: we take a level of risk daily to follow our passion for the arts and create a career from it. We are, after all, a business. The most successful jazz musicians and artists have mastered certain principles of business as they use their craft and hone it for continued success and sustainability. The pandemic gave me the chance to develop my own silver lining perspective in a different way. COVID-19 gave me the opportunity to:

1. Sit still and rest.

As a musician, so much of our net worth boils down to how busy we are, and how our creativity creates a congested schedule in order to build both exposure and income. The pandemic has allowed me to find joy and peace in sitting still and resting. It helped me to relish the quiet moments, through which I gained greater clarity about my life.

2. Be clear about what I wanted before, and what's next.

When it comes to defining success, there is often a pre-arranged script that defines what that might look like. This definition can become very separate from our own personal desires and goals. COVID-19 gave me the chance to ponder and become clear about what I want and what matters most to me.

3. Embrace activities I'd been putting off for years.

For years I've been saying to friends and colleagues that I wanted to learn ProTools (recording software), build a production studio, learn how to create my own recordings, and capture them on a higher visual level. I was able to do this, and now, because of my newly acquired space and skills, have a whole new facet to my creativity.

4. Become a better me.

I also discovered during this time that I wanted to go to graduate school to work on expanding my mind by gaining both knowledge and wisdom in an academic setting. I realized that this—now—is the time to invest in myself in a way that I hadn't before.

In conclusion, I find that the best way to deal with any difficult moment in life is to ask the divine, "What am I supposed to learn from this?" And then, once the answers are revealed, trust them and move forward in action. As always, I hope that my insights will resonate with you—in one way or another—and that you will find your way to move forward.

Acknowledgments

"And let us not grow weary in well doing, for in due season will we reap if we faint not."—Galatians 6:9

God, I thank you for peace, new ideas, and keeping my mind focused during this writing process and beyond.

Mom and Dad, you continue to be my anchors in this life, and I love you for your support during this time. Dad, thanks for letting me have your favorite chair to sit and write for hours. Iris, thanks for being a great big sister and being my biggest fan. Felicia, thanks so much for always believing in me and what you do for Don't Miss a Beat. Thank you, family (Poitiers, Sibleys, Ings, and the Herrings). Staff, kids, and parents from DMAB, thank you for your support, prayer, and love through whatever I choose to pursue. Joyce and Kennedy, thanks for your constant support always. Kendra, Kennedy, Kiaya, Liston, Jose, Deshon and Lily, Josh Alexander, I love you and thanks for your unending support.

Arlen Gargagliano, you took up this cross of a book and bore it with me equally. I could not think of a better person to partner with for this endeavor; you are simply a light of positivity in my life. Thanks to your family who shared your mind and heart with me during this undertaking, and to the incredible New Rochelle friends who supported this process as well.

Alexander Smalls, you have been a key ingredient to ushering so much wisdom, love and resources into my life. During this time of writing this book, you always knew what to say and how to advise me in the right direction, and calm my fears. Also, thank you for introducing me to the gift that is Arlen Gargagliano.

LaFredrick Coaxner, thanks for believing in all parts of me; you are my brother undoubtedly. Tawan Davis, Sterling Cummings, J'nai Bridges, and Jussie Smollett thanks for always being in my corner rooting for me. Tonya Bell, Ger Duany, Hugh Abdullah, Michael Yanover, and Alvin Clayton, thank you for your support and friendship. "Mama" Jacquie Smith, Mrs. Renee Rolfs, Audrey Hartman, and Benita Phipps, thanks for encouraging me as prayer warriors and pillars of wisdom in my life.

Chavon Sutton, thank you for believing in my writing journey enough to introduce me to Andrew Geller and start this publishing journey. Andrew, thanks for the advice that led me, and for steering me in the right direction.

Geveryl Robinson, I am thankful for the way you have believed in my writing from day one, and always challenge me to show up as my authentic self on paper.

Skyhorse Publishing Team: Tad Crawford, you are a master and kind soul that this planet needs, and your commitment to educating inquiring minds within the creative industry is so incredible and rare. To my editor, Oren Eades, thank you for your consistent support paired with your great attention to detail.

Cynthia and Walter Graham, thank you for planting that initial financial seed to make this book proposal, and writing process possible.

Mr. James and Mrs. Maxine Russell, I really appreciate your hospitality, kindness, and support during the time that I was editing this book. Our convos, cigars, beverages, and good vibes gave me energy to go back to the writing lab and create. Mosi, thanks for introducing me to the best people ever!

Thanks so much to my Florida crew: Jasmine Roberts, Taurean and Thelma Sinclair, Damien Lamar, Yhang Quintero, and Monica Turner for being incredible during this time.

Thanks to Myles and Lorraine Weinstein, and Rory Trainor, at Unlimited Myles Booking and Management. To my entertainment attorney, Justin Lynch, thank you for your support and guidance during this process and every integral move I make in business. Thank you Jerry and Joyce Fingerut, Randy and Freda Hall, David Darlington, Chris Sulit, Marcus and Jean Baylor, and Robert Sadin for your wisdom and guidance as my advisors, friends, and mentors. Stephen Duhart, thanks for being a solid and giving brother in my life.

Chloe Davis, thanks for being a supportive friend to my writing and book journey with such great advice. #thequeensenglish

Thank you Gargi Shindi (Chamber Music America) for planting that initial seed into my mind to further this entrepreneurial work. Thanks to you and Susan Dadian and Gina Izzo for believing in me and this work enough to give me the first major speaking opportunity at the "Next-Gen Conference," which was a major catalyst for me as an educator in this realm.

Johnathan Lipson, and Alec Bradley Cigars, thanks so much for giving me the right "sticks" to smoke that came in handy when I was up for hours writing. Harlem Cigar Room, thanks for allowing your place to be an office and writing lab.

Thank you Greg Knowles for introducing me to the Business of Music.

Chris Horoschak, thanks for always having my back in all things concerning graphic design in my career.

David S. Hargrett, thanks so much for always being an upright human being and so incredibly supportive to my career. I'm excited about our work together with the NAACP.

Ben Mintz, thanks for being the best CPA ever, and Jessica, for keeping my financial life organized!

Rickey Minor, for you to be someone whom I can call, text, or email was a dream of mine for many years. Thanks for being a constant voice of support in my life and career. Thanks also to Rachel and Brodie for always sharing their time with you, with me when I am around.

Wynton Marsalis, you are the epitome of greatness, and seeing you on stage at sixteen years old gave me a clear direction of what I wanted to be. Having a chance to work with you is a sheer joy and honor! Thanks for being serious and for-real about educating the next generation of musicians.

Thank you Dr. Fredara Hadley, Dr. Matthew Morrison, Dr. Courtney Bryan, Peter Martin, the Baylor Project, and Alicia Olatuja for your words in the book.

Dr. Aaron Flagg, Damien Woetzel, Barrett Hipes, and Rachel Christiansen at the Juilliard School, thanks for your support and providing a great environment for me as a student many years ago, and now as a faculty member. Dr. Jason Nicholson, and Dr. Max Matzen at Utah State University, Jennifer Rowland at Stanford University: My sincere gratitude to every institution that allowed me to lecture, and develop this work.

Adam Rose, you literally helped me at a point where I needed it in such an incredible way. I am so thankful to you and generosity, and the completion of this book is because of you. God Bless You!

Thank you to each of you who chose to purchase and read this book, may it add a blessing to each hearer and doer from the words on each page. I also pray and declare that everything your mind desires to create and manifest from the inspirations that will follow after reading this book, will allow you to succeed in time if you faint not, in due season.

I believe in the power of the prophetic word of God, and many years ago a man by the name of Apostle Earl Thomas told me that I would be an entrepreneur, write books, and do great things in business, and at that time I had no idea what that even meant. But I had the faith to believe, and now you are reading the acknowledgements in my book about entrepreneurship.

And finally, "If you believe in your heart, you'll know, just believe in yourself."

This lyric, which comes from the Broadway musical *The Wiz*, has helped me navigate many emotional moments. The song, particularly performed by Lena Horne for the motion picture soundtrack, is one that I play repeatedly. It gives me the courage to step forward, and take courage in whatever direction that I must go. I wish the same for you.

—U

#TheMusiciansCareerGuide4U

ACKNOWLEDGMENTS FROM ARLEN GARGAGLIANO

First and foremost, I thank Ulysses Owens Jr. for being who he is: oh-so-talented, generous in spirit and deed, and appreciative of all; working on this book has been an honor. Second, I thank Alexander Smalls for bringing us together, knowing—as he does so well—that we would be a great working partnership. I thank my husband Seth Markusfeld, my daughter, Sofia Markusfeld, and son, Wes Markusfeld, for their unending support and faith in me—no matter what I'm working on. To my siblings, family and friends, you know who you are—and how much I love and appreciate all you are.

And to the students reading this book, never give up. You are strong and smart. Harness your talent, dedication, and intelligence, and as my parents would say, "The sky's the limit."

Books from Allworth Press

How to Grow as a Musician
By Sheila E. Anderson (6 × 9, 264 pages, paperback, $16.99)

Your Child's Career in Music and Entertainment
By Steven C. Beer, Kathryne Badura (5.5 × 8.25, 184 pages, paperback, $14.99)

Starting Your Career as a Musician
By Neil Tortorella (6 × 9, 240 pages, paperback, $19.95)

Managing Artists in Pop Music
By Mitch Weiss, Perri Gaffney (6 × 9, 288 pages, paperback, $19.95)

Making and Marketing Music
By Jodi Summers (6 × 9, 240 pages, paperback, $19.95)

Creative Careers in Music
By Josquin Des Pres (6 × 9, 240 pages, paperback, $22.95)

Making It in the Art World
By Brainard Carey (6 × 9, 264 pages, paperback, $19.99)

Sell Online Like a Creative Genius
By Brainard Carey (6.125 × 6.12, 160 pages, paperback, $12.99)

The Profitable Artist
By New York Foundation for the Arts, Peter Cobb, Felicity Hogan, Michael Royce (6 × 9, 288 pages, paperback, $24.99)

Fund Your Dreams Like a Creative Genius
By Brainard Carey (6.13 × 6.13, 160 pages, paperback, $12.99)

Succeed with Social Media Like a Creative Genius
By Brainard Carey (6.125 × 6.125, 144 pages, paperback, $12.99)

To see our complete catalog or to order online, please visit *www.allworth.com*.